# Collins

# Grammar, Punctuation and Spelling

HarperCollins Publishers
Westerhill Road
Bishopbriggs
Glasgow
G64 2QT

First Edition 2014

Impression 10 9 8 7 6 5 4 3 2 1

© HarperCollins Publishers 2014

ISBN 978-0-00-755734-9

www.collinsdictionary.com
www.collins.co.uk

A catalogue record for this book is
available from the British Library

Typeset by Davidson Publishing
Solutions, Glasgow

Printed in Italy by Lego SpA, Lavis
(Trento)

**Editors**
Andrew Holmes
Elspeth Summers

**Design**
Steve Evans
Kevin Robbins

**Computing Support**
Thomas Callan

**For the Publisher**
Gerry Breslin
Kerry Ferguson

# Contents

# Introduction

**Collins Primary Grammar, Punctuation and Spelling** has been designed to support all pupils who are studying grammar, punctuation and spelling from age 7 to 11, whether this is for exams or to revise the key building blocks of the English language.

It contains the rules and advice that will help students get to grips with these essential aspects of the English language. There are clear, easy-to-follow explanations of how grammar works, what punctuation does, and how to spell correctly. Each section – grammar, punctuation and spelling – is laid out in an open, attractive design that guides the user easily through the information provided. Dozens of examples show exactly how the rules of English work.

The final section is a dictionary list of words that pupils must know how to spell. These have been specially selected for this age group based on real-life experience from Spelling Bees conducted by Collins Dictionaries. The words are written out in full, with their word class clearly shown, along with any other forms such as plurals, comparatives and superlatives, and inflections – all of which are also written in full, making it easy for the pupil to understand. Many helpful tips on spelling are also included throughout the spelling dictionary section to make learning easier.

**Collins Primary Grammar, Punctuation and Spelling** is an indispensable guide to the structure and rules of English, offering clear and accessible guidance for pupils from age 7 to 11.

# Grammar

## What is grammar?

Grammar is the rules of a language that tell you how to organise words to make sentences. Think about language as a series of 'blocks' that you put together. There are rules about how these blocks can be joined. The blocks are:

- the word
- the phrase
- the clause
- the sentence

This book explains what these are, how they work and how you combine them to write clear and effective English.

## Words

### Word class

Every word in a language can be sorted into a group according to what it does within a sentence. These groups are known as word classes or parts of speech. Some words can belong to a number of different word classes. This section explains what the word classes are and what they do.

### Nouns

A noun is a word that names something. In a sentence, the nouns are the words that tell you which people, places or things are involved.

There are different kinds of nouns.

#### Common nouns

These nouns are used to name every example of a certain type of thing. They start with a small letter.

| girl | city | picture |

There are three different types of common nouns.

**Words**

## Concrete nouns
A concrete noun is a physical object that you can actually touch:

donkey        bicycle        doughnut

## Abstract nouns
An abstract noun is something that does not physically exist and so cannot be touched:

happiness        beauty        imagination

## Collective nouns
A collective noun is a group or collection of things:

pack        bunch        flock

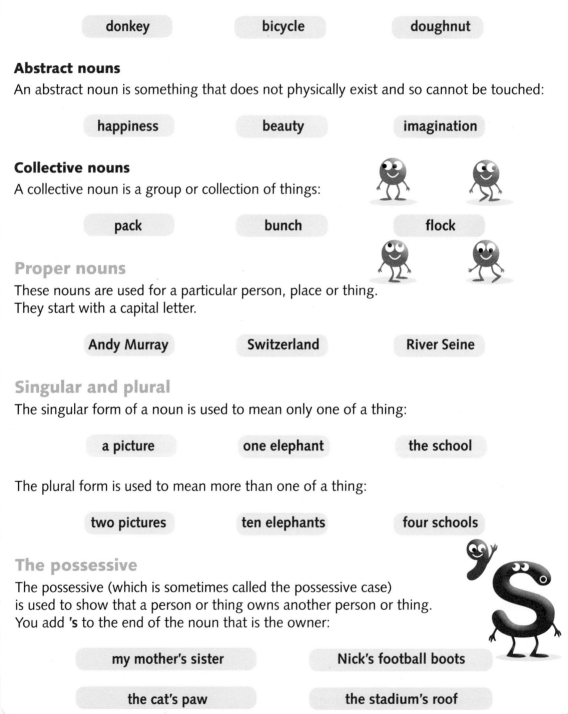

## Proper nouns
These nouns are used for a particular person, place or thing.
They start with a capital letter.

Andy Murray        Switzerland        River Seine

## Singular and plural
The singular form of a noun is used to mean only one of a thing:

a picture        one elephant        the school

The plural form is used to mean more than one of a thing:

two pictures        ten elephants        four schools

## The possessive
The possessive (which is sometimes called the possessive case)
is used to show that a person or thing owns another person or thing.
You add 's to the end of the noun that is the owner:

my mother's sister        Nick's football boots

the cat's paw        the stadium's roof

If the noun is a plural that already ends in **s**, you put an apostrophe at the end of the word:

the soldiers' uniforms

those boys' bicycles

African elephants' ears

tractors' wheels

You don't use **'s** to make a plural noun. It is only used for showing the possessive.

## Adjectives

An adjective is a word that tells you something about a noun. Adjectives can describe nouns in a number of ways:

how they feel or what they are like:

a <u>happy</u> child

a <u>strange</u> boy

a <u>joyful</u> occasion

what they look like:

a <u>large</u> tree

a <u>spotty</u> dress

a <u>gorgeous</u> beach

what they sound, smell, taste or feel like:

a <u>noisy</u> party

a <u>stinky</u> cheese

a <u>delicious</u> cake

a <u>hard</u> seat

what colour they are:

a <u>yellow</u> bag

<u>dark</u> hair

<u>green</u> leaves

where they come from:

our <u>German</u> relatives

my <u>American</u> friend

a <u>northern</u> accent

what something is made from:

<u>chocolate</u> cake

a <u>wooden</u> box

a <u>velvet</u> scarf

## Comparative Adjectives and Superlative Adjectives

When you want to make a comparison between people or things, you need to use comparative or superlative adjectives. In the examples below, **taller** is the comparative form of **tall** and **tallest** is the superlative.

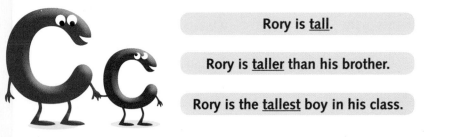

> Rory is <u>tall</u>.

> Rory is <u>taller</u> than his brother.

> Rory is the <u>tallest</u> boy in his class.

### Comparative

The comparative shows that a person or thing has more of a certain quality than another person or thing. In this case it is the quality of being tall.

You make the comparative form of an adjective by adding the suffix **-er** at the end.

> dull + -er = duller     green + -er = greener     clever + -er = cleverer

Not all comparatives are made like this, though. If the adjective is quite a long word, you use **more** instead.

> beautiful → more beautiful     eccentric → more eccentric

> interesting → more interesting

### Superlative

The superlative shows that a person or thing has the most of a certain quality out of a group of people or things.

You make the superlative form of an adjective by adding the suffix **-est** at the end.

> dull + -est = dullest     green + -est = greenest     clever + -est = cleverest

If the adjective is quite a long word, you use **most** to make the superlative.

> beautiful → most beautiful     eccentric → most eccentric

> interesting → most interesting

## Good and Bad

The adjectives **good** and **bad** don't follow the normal rules for comparative and superlative forms.

| good | better | best |
|------|--------|------|

| bad | worse | worst |
|-----|-------|-------|

There are spelling rules about adding suffixes, and you can see these on pages 81–85.

## Adverbs

An adverb is a word that tells you something about a verb. They describe the way in which something is done. Many adverbs end with the letters **-ly**.

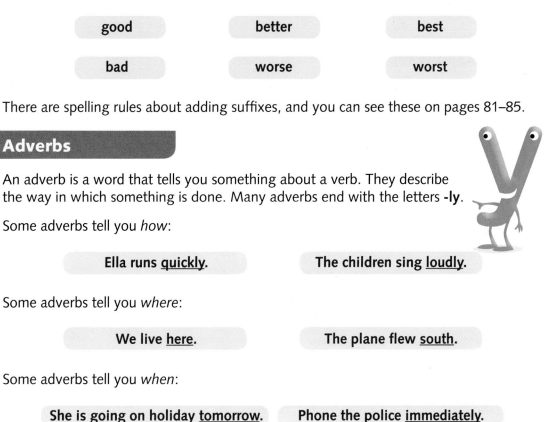

Some adverbs tell you *how*:

> Ella runs <u>quickly</u>.

> The children sing <u>loudly</u>.

Some adverbs tell you *where*:

> We live <u>here</u>.

> The plane flew <u>south</u>.

Some adverbs tell you *when*:

> She is going on holiday <u>tomorrow</u>.

> Phone the police <u>immediately</u>.

Some adverbs tell you *how much*:

> I <u>really</u> want to see that film.

> He was <u>completely</u> exhausted.

Some adverbs tell you *how often*:

> You <u>never</u> come out to play football.

> My sister and I <u>always</u> argue about who sits in the front seat of the car.

**Words**

Some adverbs go at the beginning of a sentence. These give a comment on the whole sentence:

<u>Fortunately</u>, it didn't rain.     <u>Sadly</u>, Jackie can't come on Friday.

## Prepositions

A preposition is a word that is used before a noun or a pronoun to describe how things are related or connected to each other. For example, prepositions can tell you:

- where a person or thing is:

    a cat <u>in</u> the garden     a book <u>on</u> the table     a sock <u>under</u> the bed

    Other prepositions like this include:

    above     beside     underneath     near     below

- the movement of something or someone:

    The train came <u>into</u> the station.     We pushed <u>through</u> the crowd.

    Other prepositions like this include:

    around     down     up     onto     to

- they also show how things are related in time:

    I haven't seen my auntie <u>since</u> last week.

## Conjunctions

A conjunction is a word that is used to join two words or two parts of a sentence together. There are two main types of conjunction.

### Co-ordinating conjunctions

A co-ordinating conjunction joins two things that are as important as each other:

I love fish <u>and</u> chips.

It was dry <u>so</u> I walked home.

> You can have a biscuit <u>or</u> a cake.

> She has neither mother <u>nor</u> father.

It can also show a contrast between two things:

> Joe is having a birthday party <u>but</u> he hasn't invited me.

## Subordinating conjunctions

A subordinating conjunction introduces a clause which is less important than the main part of the sentence:

> The teacher was angry <u>because</u> the pupils would not pay attention.

> Mark read his book <u>while</u> he waited for his mum to arrive.

> I must tell you some exciting news <u>before</u> we get started.

> Some dogs go a bit crazy <u>when</u> it's windy.

## Pronouns

A pronoun is a word that is used in place of a noun. You use a pronoun instead of repeating the name of a person, place or thing:

> Rachel lives next door to me. Rachel is in my class.
> > Rachel lives next door to me. <u>She</u> is in my class.

> That is the book I am reading just now. The book is very funny.
> > That is the book I am reading just now. <u>It</u> is very funny.

> I like to sit in the garden. The garden is very sunny.
> > I like to sit in the garden. <u>It</u> is very sunny.

## Personal pronouns

You use a personal pronoun instead of the subject or object of a sentence:

> <u>She</u> is good at maths.          Nobody likes <u>him</u>.

## Possessive pronouns

You use a possessive pronoun to show that something belongs to a person or thing:

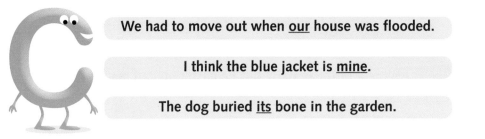

> We had to move out when <u>our</u> house was flooded.

> I think the blue jacket is <u>mine</u>.

> The dog buried <u>its</u> bone in the garden.

## Relative pronouns

You use a relative pronoun instead of a noun to join two different parts of a sentence. The relative pronouns are **who**, **whom**, **whose**, **which** and **that**. They introduce information about a noun in an earlier part of the sentence. This noun is known as the antecedent. You use **who**, **whom** and **whose** when the antecedent is a person, and **which** and **that** when it is not a person.

**who:** You use **who** when the antecedent is the subject of the second clause.

> I have an aunt <u>who</u> lives in Australia.

**whom:** You use **whom** when the antecedent is the object of the second clause.

> It was the same man <u>whom</u> we had seen earlier.

**whose:** You use **whose** to show that something belongs to the antecedent.

> Scott has a brother <u>whose</u> name is Jamie.

**which:** You use **which** when the antecedent is not a person.

> We took the road <u>which</u> leads to the sea.

**that:** You use **that** when the antecedent is not a person.

> George brought the sandwiches <u>that</u> he had made the night before.

# Grammar

## Determiners

A determiner is a word that you put in front of a noun to show more clearly what you are talking about. There are different kinds of determiners:

### Articles

The word **the** is called the definite article.

| | | |
|---|---|---|
| the robot | the traffic | the footballers |

The word **a** is called the indefinite article.

| | | |
|---|---|---|
| a caravan | a giraffe | a scooter |

If the word after **a** begins with a vowel, you use **an** instead:

| | | |
|---|---|---|
| an animal | an umbrella | an orange pencil |

### Other determiners

Other types of determiners give different information about the noun:

- the distance between the speaker and the thing they are talking about:

  <u>this</u> shoe    <u>these</u> books    <u>that</u> man    <u>those</u> houses

- who owns the thing:

  <u>my</u> bag    <u>your</u> phone    <u>his</u> kite    <u>her</u> mug

  <u>its</u> door    <u>our</u> car    <u>their</u> garden

- how much or how many:

  <u>some</u> sugar    <u>much</u> money    <u>both</u> girls

  <u>few</u> people    <u>many</u> adults    <u>several</u> birds

- the exact number:

  <u>one</u> melon    the <u>two</u> brothers    <u>fifty</u> roses    <u>ten thousand</u> years

- how something is shared out:

> **Every** child got a prize.
>
> **Each** runner is given a number.
>
> **Either** team could win on the day.
>
> **Neither** side is playing well at the moment.

## Verbs

A verb is a word that tells you about an action.

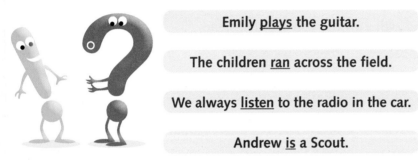

> Emily **plays** the guitar.
>
> The children **ran** across the field.
>
> We always **listen** to the radio in the car.
>
> Andrew **is** a Scout.

### Tense

The tense of a verb tells us when the action takes place.

**Present tense**

If the action is happening now, you use the present tense.
There are two types of present tense you can use:

**Simple present tense:** For this you use the verb as it is, or add an **-s** at the end:

> I **like** broccoli.
>
> You **love** peas.
>
> Max **hates** carrots.
>
> We **enjoy** swimming.
>
> Martin and Kate **play** the piano.

**Progressive present tense:** This is also known as the continuous present tense. For this you add the ending **-ing** to the verb and put a form of the verb **be** in front of it:

> I **am doing** my homework.
>
> You **are annoying** me.
>
> Lara **is painting** a picture.

**Past tense**

If the action has already happened, you use the past tense.
There are four types of past tense you can use:

**Simple past tense:** For most verbs, you add **-ed** to the end to make
the simple past tense. You add **-d** if the verb already ends in **e**:

> The children <u>screamed</u> when the lights went out.

> The dog <u>barked</u> at the postman.     I <u>scrambled</u> over the wall.

**Progressive past tense:** This is also known as the continuous past tense. You add **-ing** to
the verb and put it after **was** or **were**. You use this to talk about something that was still
happening at a certain point in the past or when something else happened:

> That was the summer when Jack and I <u>were learning</u> to ride.

> Richard <u>was cooking</u> dinner when the fire alarm went off.

**Present perfect tense:** For this you use **has** or **have** with the simple past tense of the
verb. You use the present perfect tense to show that an action has been completed:

> Abby <u>has finished</u> her project on Japan.     I <u>have baked</u> a cake for the birthday party.

**Past perfect tense:** For this you use **had** with the simple past tense of the verb. You use
this to show that something had been completed when something else happened:

> Matthew <u>had finished</u> his lunch before the others had even started.

> I <u>had packed</u> my suitcase when the taxi arrived.

**Future tense**

If the action has still to happen, you use the future tense. You do this by using **will** or
**shall** and then the verb:

> I <u>will be</u> there on time.     He says <u>he will</u> phone later today.

> We <u>shall see</u> if that's true.

## Auxiliary verbs

There are three auxiliary verbs: **be**, **have** and **do**. These are used with other verbs to make different tenses.

> I <u>was</u> washing my hair.

> The chicken <u>had</u> crossed the road.

> I <u>did</u> tidy my room eventually.

**Be**, **have** and **do** are irregular verbs, which means that they do not follow the usual rules for making verb forms.

### Be

> I <u>am</u> happy.

> You <u>are</u> sad.

> She <u>is</u> tired.

> We <u>are</u> excited.

> They <u>are</u> late.

> I <u>was</u> worried.

> You <u>were</u> angry.

> He <u>was</u> scared.

> We <u>were</u> jealous.

> They <u>were</u> sleepy.

> He is <u>being</u> silly.

> We have <u>been</u> ready for an hour.

### Have

> I <u>have</u> a cat.

> You <u>have</u> a dog.

> She <u>has</u> a rabbit.

> We <u>have</u> a parrot.

> They <u>have</u> no pets.

> I <u>had</u> an apple.

> You <u>had</u> an orange.

> He <u>had</u> a pear.

> We <u>had</u> some grapes.

> They <u>had</u> strawberries.

> Mary is <u>having</u> a baby.

> We have <u>had</u> no sleep for two days.

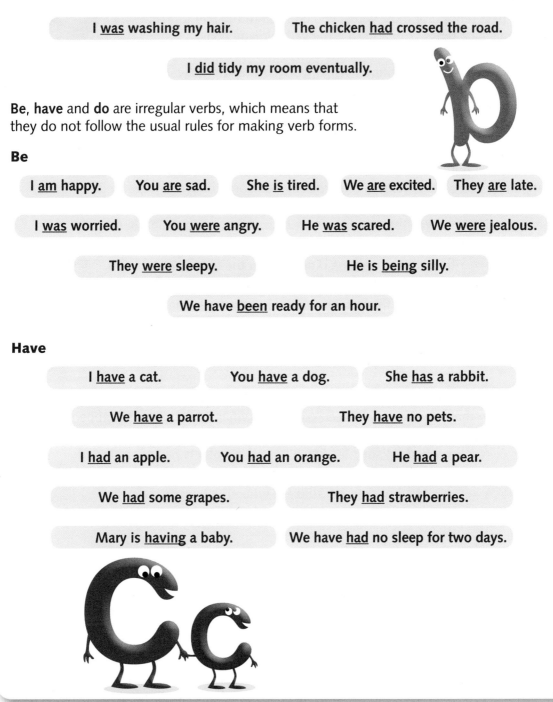

**Do**

> I <u>do</u> not like her.    You <u>do</u> not like him.    She <u>does</u> not like me.

> We <u>do</u> not like them.    They <u>do</u> not like us.

> I <u>did</u> like him.    You <u>did</u> like her.    She <u>did</u> like you.

> We <u>did</u> like them.    They <u>did</u> like him.

> The boys are <u>doing</u> their homework in their rooms.

> I have <u>done</u> what you told me.

## Modal verbs

The modal verbs are **can**, **could**, **may**, **might**, **must**, **shall**, **should**, **will**, **would** and **ought**. They are used with other verbs to add certain meanings like possibility, doubt or having to do something. Unlike all other verbs, they do not change their spellings:

> I <u>can</u> ride a bike.    Olivia <u>can</u> speak Italian.

> My friends <u>can</u> all come to my party.    I <u>could</u> be late so don't wait for me.

> You <u>may</u> be right.    I <u>might</u> go to the library after school.

> You <u>must</u> listen to the teacher.    <u>Shall</u> we take the dog for a walk?

> You <u>should</u> clean your teeth at least twice a day.

> <u>Will</u> you hang your jacket up?    I <u>would</u> love a cup of tea.

> We <u>ought</u> to leave now.

# Phrases

A phrase is a group of words which go together.

| a busy street | the family pet | very good at tennis |

Although a phrase makes sense, it is not a full sentence and needs more words to make it complete.

We live on a busy street.     The family pet is a tortoise called Bob.

My sister is very good at tennis.

## Noun phrases

A noun phrase contains at least one noun.

a tall <u>girl</u>     an extremely tall <u>girl</u>

an extremely tall <u>girl</u> with piercing blue eyes

## Adjective phrases

An adjective phrase contains at least one adjective.

a <u>brown</u> bear     a <u>big brown</u> bear

a <u>big scary brown</u> bear

## Verb phrases

A verb phrase contains an auxiliary verb and sometimes an adverb.

I <u>am enjoying</u> the summer holiday.

He <u>had been learning</u> to play the piano.

She <u>is always complaining</u> about her teachers.

## Adverb phrases

An adverb phrase tells you something about the verb. It can contain an adverb but it does not have to.

Katie tiptoed <u>very quietly</u> across the room.

The man shouted 'Fire!' <u>as loudly as possible</u>.

<u>In the morning</u>, the sky was clear.

## Preposition phrases

A preposition phrase contains a preposition and the noun that follows it.

She shut the dogs <u>in the kitchen</u>.

A plastic bag full of money was lying <u>by the side of the road</u>.

<u>At the back of the class</u>, some of the boys were laughing and telling jokes.

# Clauses

A clause is a group of words which contain a verb. There are two types of clauses.

## Main clauses

A main clause is the heart of a sentence. It would make sense if it stood on its own. Every sentence has a main clause:

> Matthew ate a cake which was covered in chocolate.

> After looking carefully in both directions, Ali crossed the road.

## Subordinate clauses

A subordinate clause is less important than the main clause. It would not make sense if it stood on its own because it is not a full sentence. It gives more information about the main clause:

> When he had looked carefully in both directions, Ali crossed the road.

> Matthew enjoyed the cake because it was covered in chocolate.

Subordinate clauses often start with **when**, **if**, **because** or **that**.

### Relative clauses

A relative clause is a type of subordinate clause. It begins with a relative pronoun: **who**, **whom**, **whose**, **which** or **that**.

> Robbie has a cat who likes fish.      David has one brother, whose name is Peter.

> Our teacher is off sick today, which is unusual for her.

You can read more about relative pronouns on page 14.

You can also write a relative clause without the relative pronoun **that** or **which**:

> She has lost the book that I lent her.      She has lost the book I lent her.

> That is the car which he has just bought.      That is the car he has just bought.

# Sentences

A sentence is a group of words that expresses an idea or describes a situation. A sentence must have:

- a capital letter at the beginning of the first word
- a full stop, a question mark or an exclamation mark at the end
- a verb

## Sentence types

A sentence can be one of four things.

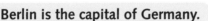

### Statement

This sentence tells you something. A statement usually starts with the subject of the sentence. It ends with a full stop:

**Berlin is the capital of Germany.**

**I am going home now.**

**It's raining.**

### Question

This sentence asks for information. It begins with a questioning word like **what**, **who**, **which**, **where**, **when**, **how** or **why**. It can also begin with a verb. It ends with a question mark:

**What is your name?**

**Have you seen my keys?**

**Where is Mount Everest?**

### Command

This sentence gives orders or instructions. You call the verb used for commands 'the imperative'. You usually put it at the start of the sentence. It can end with a full stop or, if you want to show that something is very important, an exclamation mark:

**Give me the paper.**

**Come over here.**

**Stop right there!**

If you give a polite command, the verb might not be at the start of the sentence:

> Please stop talking.

## Exclamation

This sentence expresses a strong feeling. It ends with an exclamation mark:

> What a laugh!

> You're here at last!

> I never want to see you again!

# Sentence structure

There are different types of sentences which can be grouped by how the sentence is written.

## Simple sentence

A simple sentence contains just one main clause:

> Zoya threw the ball.

> Today is my birthday.

## Compound sentence

A compound sentence contains two or more main clauses joined by a conjunction:

> Zoya threw the ball and Marion caught it.

> Today is my birthday but my party is tomorrow.

## Complex sentence

A complex sentence has a main clause and one or more subordinate clauses:

> Zoya threw the ball to Marion, who was standing on the other side of the pitch.

> Today is my birthday, although my party isn't until tomorrow, which is a pity.

## Parts of the sentence

Sentences contain a number of parts.

### Subject

The subject is the person or thing that does the action in a sentence. It is a noun, a noun phrase or a pronoun. It comes before the verb.

<u>Louise</u> fell asleep.

<u>Dogs</u> don't like fireworks.

<u>The red car</u> is parked on the other side of the road.

<u>She</u> threw a cushion across the room.

### Verb

A sentence must have a verb or a verb phrase.

The man <u>walks</u> slowly up the hill.

Jessica <u>fainted</u>.

Adam <u>is having</u> a haircut.

People <u>have lived</u> in this place for hundreds of years.

### Object

The object is the person or thing that has the action of the verb done to it. It is a noun, a noun phrase or a pronoun. It comes after the verb. Not all sentences have an object.

Kim loves <u>chocolate</u>.

I have lost <u>my new green rucksack</u>.

Are you going to ask <u>him</u> to the prom?

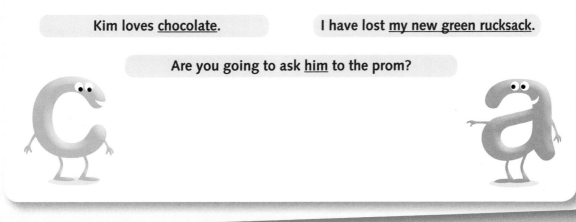

## Complement

A complement is a word or phrase that tells you something about the subject of the sentence. It is a noun, a noun phrase, an adjective or an adjective phrase. Not all sentences have a complement. The verbs **be**, **become**, **feel** and **seem** need a complement.

> Laura is <u>an architect</u>.

> They became <u>very good friends</u> when they worked together.

> The boys felt <u>silly</u> when they had to dress up.

> She seems <u>perfectly happy</u>.

## Adverbial

An adverbial can be an adverb, an adverb phrase, a preposition clause or a subordinate clause. It tells you something about how the action in the sentence is happening, for example when it is happening, where it is happening, how it is happening, how often it is happening or why it is happening. Not all sentences have adverbials.

> <u>Suddenly</u>, it started to rain <u>heavily</u>.

> <u>Breathing quietly</u>, Lee crept out of the room.

> You probably won't notice it <u>after a while</u>.

> I'll make a cup of tea <u>when I've finished reading this</u>.

An adverbial can go anywhere in a sentence:

> I <u>greatly</u> admire your courage.

> The door closed <u>with a loud bang</u>.

> <u>Honestly</u>, I didn't mean to be rude to you.

When the adverbial is at the start of the sentence it is called a fronted adverbial. These are followed by a comma:

> **<u>Seriously</u>, are you wearing that?**

> **<u>At the end of the match</u>, the players shook hands.**

> **<u>Bitterly disappointed</u>, the home supporters left the stadium quickly.**

> **<u>When the cake is golden brown</u>, take it out of the oven.**

## Active voice and passive voice

There are two different ways of presenting the same information in a sentence. These are the active voice and the passive voice. In the active voice, the subject of the sentence does the action:

> **Nina is feeding the rabbit.**
> subject   verb

> **The cat chased a mouse.**
> subject  verb

In the passive voice, the subject of the sentence has the action done to it:

> **The rabbit is being fed by Nina.**
> subject     verb

> **The mouse was chased by a cat.**
> subject      verb

The passive voice uses **be** with the past participle of the verb:

> **is being fed**

> **was chased**

It usually sounds more natural to use the active voice when you are writing, but sometimes it is good to use the passive voice if you do not know who did something or you do not want to blame someone.

> **The bus shelter has been vandalised.**

> **The front door has been left open again.**

# Making words

English is very good at making new words from existing words. This can be done by putting words together or by adding prefixes and suffixes.

## Prefixes

A prefix is a letter or group of letters that is added to the beginning of a word to make a new word. Adding a prefix to a word changes the word's meaning. When you write a prefix on its own, you put a hyphen after it, for example **un-**. When you add the prefix to a word to make a new word, you do not keep the hyphen (except in a very few cases which you can see on pages 56–57):

> **un- + usual = unusual**
> **un- + cover = uncover**
> **un- + happiness = unhappiness**

The prefix **un-** means 'not' so when you add it to a word you give it the opposite meaning:

> **un- + friendly = unfriendly (not friendly)**

Other prefixes that do this are **dis-**, **non-** and **in-**:

> **dis- + agree = disagree**
> **non- + fiction = nonfiction**
> **in- + expensive = inexpensive**

When you put **in-** before words that begin with certain letters, the **n** changes:

- before **l**, **in-** changes to **il-**: **il- + legal = illegal**
- before **m**, **in-** changes to **im-**: **im- + modest = immodest**
- before **p**, **in-** changes to **im-**: **im- + patient = impatient**
- before **r**, **in-** changes to **ir-**: **ir- + rational = irrational**

# Grammar

Other prefixes that are useful to know are:

| prefix | meaning | example | language it comes from |
|---|---|---|---|
| anti- | against | anticlockwise | *Greek* |
| pro- | in favour of | prowar | *Latin* |
| de- | undo or remove | defrost | *Latin* |
| bi- | two or twice | bimonthly | *Latin* |
| auto- | self | autobiography | *Greek* |
| ante- | before | antenatal | *Latin* |
| co- | together | cooperate | *Latin* |
| pre- | before | predate | *Latin* |
| re- | again | reheat | *Latin* |
| circum- | round or about | circumference | *Latin* |
| ex- | out or outside of | external | *Latin* |
| inter- | between | international | *Latin* |
| mis- | wrong or false | misbehave | *Old English* |
| sub- | under | subway | *Latin* |
| super- | larger, over or beyond | superpower | *Latin* |
| mini- | small | miniskirt | *English* |
| over- | too much | overeat | *English* |
| trans- | across | transmit | *Latin* |
| tele- | distant | television | *Greek* |
| ultra- | extremely | ultramodern | *Latin* |
| micro- | small | microcomputer | *Greek* |
| tri- | three | tricycle | *Latin* |

## Suffixes

A suffix is a letter or group of letters that is added to the end of a word to make a new word. Adding a suffix to a word changes a word's meaning. When you write a suffix on its own, you put a hyphen in front of it, for example **-ness**. When you add the suffix to a word to make a new word, you do not keep the hyphen:

> sad + -ness = sadness

There are spelling rules about adding suffixes to words. You can find these on pages 81–85.

Two useful suffixes are **-ful** and **-less**. These are added to words to make adjectives. The suffix **-ful** means 'full of', while **-less** means 'without':

> hope + -ful = hopeful (full of hope)

> hope + -less = hopeless (without hope)

> pain + -ful = painful (full of pain)

> pain + -less = painless (without pain)

Here are some other suffixes that make adjectives:

| suffix | meaning | example |
|--------|---------|---------|
| -able | able to | readable |
| -al | related to | traditional |
| -ary | related to | revolutionary |
| -ible | able to | reversible |
| -ic | related to | rhythmic |
| -ish | fairly or rather | smallish |
| -ist | prejudiced | racist |
| -ive | tending to | divisive |
| -like | resembling | dreamlike |
| -ous | full of | perilous |
| -y | like or full of | grassy |

# Grammar

There are some suffixes that mean 'the state of', 'the condition of' or 'the quality of'. These make nouns:

| suffix | example |
|--------|---------|
| -ness | blind + -ness = blindness |
| -ity | stupid + -ity = stupidity |
| -ance | accept + -ance = acceptance |
| -ation | legalize + -ation = legalization |
| -dom | bore +- dom = boredom |
| -ence | depend + ence = dependence |
| -hood | child + -hood = childhood |
| -ion | elect + -ion = election |
| -ship | dictator + -ship = dictatorship |

Other suffixes that make nouns include:

| suffix | meaning | example |
|--------|---------|---------|
| -er | person who does something | painter |
| -er | thing that does something | fastener |
| -er | person from a place | islander |
| -ant | person who does something | defendant |
| -ism | action or condition | criticism |
| -ism | prejudice | sexism |
| -ment | state of having | employment |
| -ology | study of | biology |

Suffixes that make verbs include:

| suffix | meaning | example |
|--------|---------|---------|
| -ate | become or take on | hyphenate |
| -ise or -ize | change or affect | motorise |
| -ify | make or become | purify |
| -en | make or become | dampen |

To make an adverb from an adjective you add the suffix **-ly**, which means 'in this way':

> kind + -ly = kindly
>
> proper + -ly = properly
>
> real + -ly = really
>
> week + -ly = weekly

## Root Words

A root word is word which can stand alone and still make sense, for example **read**. You can add prefixes and suffixes to a root word in order to make new words:

> read   reads   reading   reader   readable   misread   reread

## Compound Words

A compound word is one that is made from two or more root words. Lots of English words are made in this way.

> girl + friend = girlfriend
>
> soft + ware = software
>
> after + shave = aftershave

Compound words can be written in different ways:

- as one word:   bookcase   wallpaper   outrun   skateboard
- as two words:   post office   fire engine   eye shadow   Roman Catholic
- with a hyphen:   bone-dry   one-way   face-lift   middle-of-the-road

## Word Families

A word family is a group of words that are related to each other because they come from the same root word.

> sign   signature   signage   signify   significant   signpost   signal
> undersign   design   designate

> solve   solver   solvent   soluble   solution   dissolve   resolve

# Writing good English

Once you know how sentences are made, you can start to put them together to make longer pieces of writing. A group of sentences together is called a paragraph.

## Paragraphs

You start a paragraph on a new line. A paragraph contains one idea or one part of an argument. When you want to introduce another idea or another part of an argument, you start a new paragraph:

> More British households have dogs than any other pets. A survey has found that 25% of homes in the UK have a dog. The labrador retriever remains the most popular dog, followed by the cocker spaniel and springer spaniel.

> Cats are the next most popular pet in the country, being found in 19% of British homes. The favourite breed by far is the shorthair domesticated cat, although the Siamese, Burmese and Persian are all increasing in popularity.

If you are quoting direct speech, you start a new paragraph for each new speaker.

> "Are you playing in the match after school today?" asked Nathan.
>
> "No," replied Simon. "I have to go to the dentist."

If you are writing a story, each new event in the story should have its own paragraph. You do, however, need to link paragraphs to bring your writing together. This is called cohesion. If a piece of writing has cohesion then it all joins together smoothly.

## Cohesion

There are a number of ways to add cohesion to your writing.

### Use of tense

You need to keep your tenses consistent in a piece of work. This means that if you start off in the present tense, you keep to the present tense all the way through. If you start in the past tense, keep to the past tense.

Zack *is* nervous. He *has* to sing a solo at the school concert next week. He *is* worried that he will forget the words or sing out of tune. The teacher *tells* him that he will be fine.

## Cohesive devices

These are words that connect different parts of the text. These include:

### Determiners

We went to the pond to feed the ducks. <u>They</u> swam towards us eagerly.
(**They** links with **the ducks** in the first sentence)

I really enjoyed my school days. <u>Those</u> were the best days of my life.
(**Those** links with **school days**)

### Pronouns

The runners are ready to go. <u>They</u> are waiting for the starting pistol.
(**They** links with **the runners**)

I don't like my maths teacher. <u>He</u> shouts a lot.
(**He** links with **my maths teacher**)

### Conjunctions

I will need to save up some money <u>before</u> I can buy a new phone.
(**before** shows time relationship)

Please let me know <u>when</u> you want to go home.
(**when** shows time relationship)

### Adverbs

I clean my teeth. <u>Then</u> I get dressed. ('Then' shows time relationship)

I get dressed. <u>Next</u> I make my lunch. ('Next' shows time relationship)

### Connectives

Conjunctions and adverbs are also known as connectives. They connect ideas between clauses and sentences.

I am scared of horses. <u>Nevertheless</u>, I am going riding tomorrow.

We are moving house. <u>Therefore</u> I will be changing schools.

Some other connectives are:

later    afterwards    previously

similarly    furthermore    moreover    on the other hand

in contrast    however    meanwhile

### Ellipsis

Ellipsis is missing out a word or phrase that you would normally include. By doing this, you can link clauses and sentences.

Do you like jazz? I don't like it.
> Do you like jazz? I don't.

Julie looked behind and she started run.
> Julie looked behind and started to run.

Ellipsis is also the name of a punctuation mark. You can see more about this on page 58.

# Ambiguity

Ambiguity is when something is not clear and could confuse the reader. For example:

The dog bit the man and he barked.

Who barked? The man or the dog?

The dog bit the man and then barked.

By removing the pronoun **he** and adding the adverb **then**, you get rid of the ambiguity.

# Avoiding repetition

You use pronouns to avoid repeating nouns in a piece of writing.

My aunt lives in Rome. My aunt has lived there for twenty years. My aunt works as a translator.

> My aunt lives in Rome. <u>She</u> has lived there for twenty years. <u>She</u> works as a translator.

## Expressing possibility

You can express the idea of possibility or uncertainty in two ways.

### Modal verbs

You can use verbs like **may**, **might**, **could** and **should** to show that something is not certain.

> We <u>may</u> be getting a puppy.

> I <u>might</u> not be here when you get home.

> The team <u>could</u> be moving to a new stadium.

> Robert <u>should</u> be able to meet you at the station.

### Adverbs

You can also use certain adverbs to show that something is not definite.

> <u>Maybe</u> we can go next week.

> <u>Perhaps</u> you can help me with this?

> She is <u>possibly</u> too late to join the class now.

## Types of English

The way you talk to your friends is not the same way that you talk to your head teacher. We write and speak in different ways, depending on the situation.

### Informal language

This is how you write to friends or close family, for example in emails or texts:

> Hey how R U? Soz i missed ur call. @ lazergame with jack n anna.
> It was beast! cant wait 2 go again. I'll phone u l8r. ☺

Some features of informal language:

- slang words (**beast**)
- contracted forms (**I'll**)

- abbreviations (**R U**, **soz**, **ur**, **n**)
- smileys or emoticons (☺)
- lack of punctuation (**jack**, **anna**, **cant**, **i**)
- informal greeting (**Hey**)
- short simple sentences
- simple vocabulary
- numbers or symbols (**2** for **to**, **@** for **at** or **l8r** for **later**)

## Question tags

A question tag is a short question at the end of a statement. They are used to check that the listener agrees with the speaker. They are common in speech and informal writing but you should use not them in formal writing:

> You've cleaned your room, <u>haven't you</u>?

> We're not going to that, <u>are we</u>?

## Formal language

This is the language you should use when you are writing things for school.

> **Dear Mrs Jenkins**
>
> **I am sorry I missed your telephone call yesterday. I was out with two of my friends, Jack and Anna. We were at an attraction called Lazergame, where you chase and shoot each other with lasers. It was really good fun and I am hoping to go again soon.**
>
> **I will see you at five o'clock on Friday, assuming your train is on time.**
>
> **Yours sincerely, Eve**

Some of the features of formal language:

- full forms (**I am**, **you are**, **I will**)
- use of punctuation (**I**, **Lazergame**, **Jack**, **Anna**)
- no slang (**sorry** not **soz**)
- longer, more complex sentences
- formal opening and closing (**Dear**, **Yours sincerely**)
- more difficult words (**attraction**, **assuming**)
- Not using symbols instead of words

## Formal and informal vocabulary

You should avoid informal and slang words in your written work, unless you are writing conversation. For example, use:

**child** (not **kid**)    **man** (not **guy**)    **friend** (not **pal**)

**satisfactory** (not **OK**)    **angry** (not **ballistic**)    **wealthy** (not **minted**)

**relax** (not **chill**)    **impressive** (not **awesome**)

**very good** (not **well good**)

## Subjunctive

Another feature of formal language is the subjunctive. This is a form of verb that is sometimes used to show the possibility of something happening or the wish for it to happen. You use **were** instead of **was**:

If your father <u>were</u> here he would help you.

If I <u>were</u> rich I would buy a house like that.

Susan has always wished she <u>were</u> taller.    I wouldn't do that if I <u>were</u> you.

# Standard English and Non-standard English

Standard English is the form that you learn to read and write in school. It is the language that you read in newspapers and books, and hear on the television and radio news. It obeys the rules of English grammar and can be spoken in any accent. You should use this for anything you write in school and in official letters and emails. Non-standard English is the language that people often speak, where they don't always follow the rules of grammar. You should avoid using this in writing.

**Tense agreement**

You must make sure that you do not jump between tenses when you are writing. If you start off in the past tense, keep to the past tense.

I was walking down the street when I <u>saw</u> my friend coming towards me.
(NOT I was walking down the street when I <u>see</u> my friend coming towards me.)

# Grammar

## Subject and verb agreement

You must use the correct form of the verb for the subject of the sentence.

> **He <u>was</u> asleep when the fire broke out.**
> (NOT **He <u>were</u> asleep when the fire broke out.**)

> **We were happy to hear the news. (NOT We was happy to hear the news.)**

## Verb inflections

You must use the correct verb form for the past tense of irregular verbs. Some verbs (irregular verbs) have two different forms for the past tense, for example **see**. These are called the past tense and the past participle. The past tense is the one that makes the simple past of the verb. The past participle is the one you use with **have**.

> **I <u>saw</u> = the past tense**

> **I have <u>seen</u> = the past participle**

> **I <u>saw</u> him yesterday. (NOT I <u>seen</u> him yesterday.)**

> **You should have <u>gone</u> to bed earlier. (NOT You should have <u>went</u> to bed earlier.)**

> **He <u>did</u> his homework in school. (NOT He <u>done</u> his homework in school.)**

Also, you should write **I was sitting** not **I was sat**:

> **I was <u>sitting</u> on the wall when Zain appeared.**
> (NOT **I was <u>sat</u> on the wall when Zain appeared.**)

## Verb contractions

Some shortened forms of verbs are used in non-standard English. You should not use them in your writing:

- **ain't = am not, are not, is not**   **He <u>is not</u> here yet. (NOT He <u>ain't</u> here yet.)**

- **amn't = am not**   **I <u>am not</u> going. (NOT I <u>amn't</u> going.)**

- shouldnt've = should not have

> You <u>should not have</u> done that.
> (NOT You <u>shouldnt've</u> done that.)

- innit = is it not?

## I and me

You must not confuse **I** and **me**. You use **I** for the subject of the sentence, and **me** for the object.

> Helen and <u>I</u> are going swimming. (NOT Helen and <u>me</u> are going swimming.)

> Kevin threw the water balloon at Linda and <u>me</u>.
> (NOT Kevin threw the water balloon at Linda and <u>I</u>.)

If you are not sure whether to use **I** or **me** in a sentence like this, take the other person out of the sentence and see if it still makes sense:

> Helen and I are going swimming.
> > <u>I</u> am going swimming. (NOT <u>Me</u> is going swimming.)

> Kevin threw the water balloon at Linda and me.
> > Kevin threw the water balloon at <u>me</u>. (NOT Kevin threw the water balloon at <u>I</u>.)

## Double negatives

A negative is a word like **not**, **nor**, **never** or **nothing**, which means **no**. Sometimes people use two of these in sentence and this is known as a double negative. You should not do this in standard English:

> I did<u>n't</u> have any money.
> (NOT I did<u>n't</u> have <u>no</u> money.)

> We have <u>never</u> been there.
> (NOT We have<u>n't</u> <u>never</u> been there.)

> He did<u>n't</u> do anything wrong.
> (NOT He did<u>n't</u> do <u>nothing</u> wrong.)

## Reporting speech

There are two ways of dealing with speech when you are writing.

### Direct speech

This is when you quote exactly what a person says. For this you use inverted commas and verbs like **say**, **reply**, **answer**, **mutter** and **shout**. If you are showing a conversation you start a new paragraph every time a different person speaks.

> "Hello, Sarah," said Mike. "What are you doing here?"
>
> "I'm meeting my friends here," she replied. "We are having lunch and then we are going to the cinema to see the new Hunger Games film."
>
> "Who's all going?" asked Mike.
>
> Sarah said, "Lucy, Aila, Rachel and Fiona."

### Indirect speech

This is when you report what a person has said but do not quote it exactly. You do not use inverted commas for this, and you do not use question marks or exclamation marks.

> Mike asked Sarah what she was doing in the cafe. She told him she was meeting her friends for lunch and then going to the cinema. Mike asked who was going and Sarah told him it was Lucy, Aila, Rachel and Fiona.

# Synonyms

You should try to use a wide range of words in your writing. It is good to avoid repeating the same words again and again. You can do this by using synonyms of overused words. A synonym is a word that means the same as another word. If you are writing a story about a conversation, instead of using **said** each time, you could use **mentioned**, **responded**, **muttered**, **whispered** or **snapped**. By doing this, you make your writing more interesting and entertaining.

Here are some words to avoid and some synonyms you could try instead:

* **nice**:

| attractive | charming | agreeable | delightful |
|---|---|---|---|

| pleasant | likeable | pleasurable |
|---|---|---|

* **great**:

| excellent | outstanding | superb |
|---|---|---|

| skilful | first-rate | tremendous |
|---|---|---|

* **look**:

| glance | peek | gaze | stare | watch |
|---|---|---|---|---|

| survey | examine | study | gape |
|---|---|---|---|

* **big**:

| gigantic | immense | massive |
|---|---|---|

| vast | enormous | colossal |
|---|---|---|

Be careful, though. A word that is a synonym for one meaning of a word might not work for another. You can replace **good** with **well-behaved** in the phrase 'a good child', but **well-behaved** does not work instead of **good** in 'a good book'.

# Antonyms

An antonym is a word that means the opposite of another word. For example **forget** is the antonym of **remember**.

You can use antonyms to show a contrast:

> William had hoped by now to be <u>rich</u>; he was shocked to realise he was actually rather <u>poor</u>.

> After so many years her <u>love</u> had turned to <u>hate</u>.

You can use an antonym with a negative to emphasise something that might seem surprising:

> Maria was <u>not unhappy</u> that the party had been cancelled.
> (Maria was actually happy about it)

> This government policy is <u>not unpopular</u> with the public.
> (The policy is actually popular)

Only use a word if you are certain that you know what it means. If you are not sure, check the meaning in a good dictionary. For synonyms and antonyms, you should check a thesaurus.

# Layout

When you are writing something for school, think about the way it appears on the page. Is it clear and easy to read? The layout is important. You must break your writing into paragraphs, but there are other things you can do to make your work readable.

## Headings

A heading comes at the very top of the page before you write anything else. It tells the reader the title of the story or report. You can put this in a larger type size than the rest of the document if you like. It is often typed in bold.

## Subheadings

If there are sections within the piece of writing, you can give each of these a subheading. It can be in bold or underlined.

## Columns

You can put lists of information into columns, each with a heading.

## Bullet points

You can also show lists with bullet points (see more on bullet points on page 57).

Here's an example of good layout:

---

### Emblems of the United States of America

**Background**

Each of the 50 states that make up the United States of America has three emblems to represent it. These are a bird, a flower and a tree. These are usually, if not always, native to the state.

**History**

The first state flower was selected in 1892 when Washington chose the coast rhododendron as its emblem. Texas was the first to select a state tree – the pecan – in 1919. In 1927, seven states (Alabama, Florida, Maine, Missouri, Oregon, Texas and Wyoming) chose the birds that they wanted as their state emblems.

| State | State Bird | State Tree | State Flower |
| --- | --- | --- | --- |
| Alabama | yellowhammer | longleaf pine | camellia |
| Alaska | willow ptarmigan | sitka spruce | forget-me-not |
| Arizona | cactus wren | blue palo verde | saguaro cactus blossom |
| Arkansas | mockingbird | loblolly pine | apple blossom |
| California | California quail | coast redwood | California poppy |
| Colorado | lark bunting | Colorado blue spruce | Rocky Mountain columbine |

**Other US territories with state emblems:**

- Guam
- Northern Marianas
- Puerto Rico
- US Virgin Islands

---

# Punctuation

## What is punctuation?

Punctuation is the use of marks in writing to make it easier to read and understand. These marks are called punctuation marks.

The punctuation marks you need to know are: full stop, question mark, exclamation mark, comma, apostrophe, inverted comma, bracket, dash, semicolon, colon, hyphen, bullet point and ellipsis. These are all explained in the following pages.

Here are some basic things to remember when you write:

* Leave a space between each word.
* Start each sentence with a capital letter.
* Finish each sentence with a full stop, a question mark or an exclamation mark.

## Letters

Letters are written symbols which go together to make words. An alphabet is a set of these letters.

### Small letters

The English alphabet has 26 letters:

a b c d e f g h i j k l m n o p q r s t u v w x y z

When you write letters in that way, they are called small letters (also known as lower case letters). Most words are written in small letters.

### Capital letters

A capital letter (which is also sometimes just called a capital) is a way of writing a letter of the alphabet. Each letter can be written as a small letter or a capital letter. Here is the alphabet in capital letters.

A B C D E F G H I J K L M N O P Q R S T U V W X Y Z

## When should you use a capital letter in your writing?

There are a number of places where you should make the first letter of a word a capital.

- At the beginning of a sentence:

Phone me when you are ready to come home.

What is the name of that band you want to see?

The fire alarm rang so we all had to leave the building.

- For the names of people and places:

| | | |
|---|---|---|
| Jessica Ennis | Prince William | Robert Muchamore |
| Birmingham | Cuba | Kilimanjaro |

- For nationalities and languages:

| | | |
|---|---|---|
| Spanish | Iraqi | Nigerian |
| Italian | Urdu | Russian |

- For the days of the week and months of the year:

| | | |
|---|---|---|
| Wednesday | Friday | Sunday |
| January | April | November |

- For religions and religious festivals:

| | | |
|---|---|---|
| Buddhism | Islam | Sikhism |
| Diwali | Easter | Yom Kippur |

- For the names of companies and products:

| | | |
|---|---|---|
| Pepsi | Apple | Adidas |
| Converse | Pringles | Dairy Milk |

# Punctuation

- For the names of books, TV programmes, films, plays, magazines, newspapers and websites:

  | Catching Fire | Horrible Histories | Despicable Me |
  |---|---|---|
  | Macbeth | First News | Amazon |

- For the pronoun I:

  Hashim and I are in the same English class.

  I forgot to bring my gym kit to school today.

  What should I give Lucy for her birthday?

## Full stop

The full stop is a dot like . When you are writing a full stop, you put it so that it sits just on top of the line.

### When should you use a full stop in your writing?

- At the end of a sentence:

  My friends and I are going skating tomorrow.

  I love dogs but I'm scared of cats.

  Remind me to post that letter.

- At the end of a word or phrase that can stand on its own:

  | Sorry. | Good morning. | Do you like rap? Not much. |
  |---|---|---|

You do not put a full stop at the end of a question or an exclamation but you do if you are writing *about* a question or exclamation:

The man asked me where the nearest shop was. ("Where is the nearest shop?" asked the man.)

She screamed that she hated me. ("I hate you!" she screamed.)

## Question mark

The question mark is a symbol that looks like **?** You put it at the end of a sentence. When you are writing a question mark, you put the dot just above the line.

### When should you use a question mark in your writing?

You use a question mark to show that you are asking a direct question:

**Did I leave my skateboard at your house?**

**Where do you live?**

**Do you want to go swimming tomorrow?**

## Exclamation mark

The exclamation mark is a symbol that looks like **!** You put it at the end of a sentence. When you are writing an exclamation mark, you put the dot just above the line.

### When should you use an exclamation mark in your writing?

- To show a strong feeling like anger, surprise or excitement:

    **I can't believe you said that!**

    **We're getting a puppy!**

    **You scared me!**

- When you are telling someone to do something:

    **Don't touch that!**

    **Pass the ball to me!**

    **Close the door after you!**

## Comma

The comma is a mark that looks like **,** which you write or type. When you are writing a comma, it should sit just on the line, with its tail hanging down across the line.

### When should you use a comma in your writing?

- To separate items in a list, instead of repeating the word **and**:

> **We need to pack shorts, t-shirts, a swimsuit and trainers.**

> **For this cake you only need eggs, milk, sugar and flour.**

> **You can contact me by phone, email or text message.**

- To mark a short pause between different parts of a sentence:

> **Most people like summer best, but I prefer winter.**

> **After a month of rain, the sun finally came out.**

> **Unfortunately, this year's school trip to France has been cancelled.**

> **The week after next, we are moving house.**

- To separate the name of the person or people you are talking to from the rest of the sentence:

> **Are you coming to the party, Rachel?**

> **Good evening, ladies and gentlemen.**

- If the name is in the middle of the sentence, there should be a comma before and after it:

> **I'd like to start, boys and girls, by introducing myself.**

> **Can you tell me, Helen, what you are doing here?**

**Comma**

- When you are quoting someone:

> "I have never been in this shop before," said Emily.

> Anum replied, "We come here after school every Friday."

Where you put the comma depends on the way the sentence is written. If it ends with a verb (**said**) and the speaker (**Emily**), the comma should be inside the inverted commas. If the sentence begins with the speaker (**Anum**) and the verb (**replied**), the comma comes after the verb and before the inverted commas.

For the first type of example, you do not need a comma if the quotation ends in an exclamation mark or question mark:

> "Come here quickly!" she yelled.

> "Who's your English teacher this year?" asked Matthew.

But you do still need a comma for the second:

> The boy shouted, "There's a fire!"

> Linda asked, "Do you want to go to the pictures on Saturday?"

- To mark off separate information that is not essential:

> Andy raced down the street, jumping over a giant puddle on the pavement, and reached the bus just as it was starting to move away from the stop.

You could take out the words within the commas and this sentence would still make sense. Putting information in commas in this way is called parenthesis.

> Andy raced down the street and reached the bus just as it was starting to move away from the stop.

# Apostrophe

The apostrophe is a mark that looks like **'** which you use when you are writing or typing. When you are writing an apostrophe, you put it at the top of the letter, for example **Eve's bike** or **the witch's cat**.

## When should you use an apostrophe in your writing?

There are two reasons for using an apostrophe: possession and contraction.

- Possession: Apostrophes show possession or ownership of something:

    **Jane's phone**                 **the teachers' cloakroom**

- When you want to show that something belongs to a single person, place or thing, you add **'s** to the end of the person, place or thing:

    **Callum's bag (the bag belonging to Callum)**

    **Britain's castles (the castles found in Britain)**

    **the car's windscreen (the windscreen on the car)**

If the person, place or thing ends in **s**, just add **'**:

    **James' hat**                 **Paris' streets**

- When you want to show that something belongs to more than one person, place or thing, you add **'** after the word, but you do this only if the word ends in **s**:

    **the players' uniforms (the uniforms belonging to the players)**

    **the islands' ferry (the ferry that goes to the islands)**

    **the trees' leaves (the leaves on the trees)**

- If the plural of a word does not end in s, you add **'s** to show possession:

    **the children's jotters (the jotters belonging to the children)**

    **the teeth's enamel (the enamel on teeth)**

    **mice's whiskers (the whiskers that mice have)**

**Apostrophe**

- Contraction: Apostrophes show that a letter (or more than one letter) has been removed:

  can't          I'll          he'd

This is called a contraction; two words are joined together and a letter, or some letters, are dropped.

Here are some of the commonest contractions:

| had or would | will or shall | have | be |
|---|---|---|---|
| I'd = I had or I would | I'll = I will or I shall | I've = I have | I'm = I am |
| you'd = you had or you would | you'll = you will | you've = you have | you're = you are |
| she'd = she had or she would | she'll = she will | she's = she has | she's = she is |
| they'd = they had or they would | they'll = they will | they've = they have | they're = they are |

Here are some contractions with **not**:

| do | be | have | will | would | can | could | should |
|---|---|---|---|---|---|---|---|
| don't | aren't | haven't | won't | wouldn't | can't | couldn't | shouldn't |
| doesn't | isn't | hasn't | | | | | |
| didn't | wasn't | hadn't | | | | | |
| | weren't | | | | | | |

# Punctuation

## Inverted comma

Inverted commas are marks which are put before and after words to show exactly what someone is saying. They are also known as speech marks or quotation marks, and they look like " " or ' '. When you are writing inverted commas, you put them at the top of the letters.

### When should you use inverted commas in your writing?

To show exactly what a person said or is saying:

**"You can all go home early," said the teacher.**

**Her mother asked, "Can you please take the dog for a walk?"**

This is called direct speech. When you write direct speech you should put the punctuation at the end of the speech inside the inverted commas:

**"Help me!" cried the man.**

**Jenny said, "I'm sorry I can't come to your party."**

## Bracket

Brackets are punctuation marks that are used in pairs. They are usually like ( ) and these are sometimes known as round brackets. Sometimes people use square brackets which look like [ ].

### When should you use brackets in your writing?

Brackets are used to contain things that have been added to give extra information. The sentence would still make sense without the words inside the brackets. Putting information in brackets in this way is called parenthesis.

**My grandmother (my mother's mother) was born in Dundee.**

**Bring something good to eat (like chocolate, crisps or popcorn) to the sleepover on Saturday.**

**Miss Brown (I mean my maths teacher, not Miss Brown who works in the office) is getting married next month.**

# Dash

The dash is a mark that is a short line – which is longer than a hyphen. When you are writing a dash, you put it above the line, about halfway between the top and the bottom of the letters beside it. You should also put a space before and after a dash.

## When should you use a dash in your writing?

You use a dash for two different things:

- To show a break in a sentence:

> **Don't leave your plate there – put it back in the kitchen.**

> **I'm not sure – what was the question again?**

> **Bring me my bag please – the grey one.**

- To mark off separate information:

> **Peter and I – the others can't make it – are going skating on Sunday.**

> **We are collecting books – it doesn't matter whether they are old or new – for the school sale.**

> **To make a smoothie you put ice, milk, yoghurt and fruit – raspberries and strawberries are good – and mix them all in a blender.**

This is called parenthesis. You put a dash before and after the extra information.

## Semicolon

The semicolon is a mark that looks like ; (a full stop directly above a comma). When you are writing a semicolon, you put the comma part on top of the line, with the tail hanging across the line.

### When should you use a semicolon in your writing?

- To separate items in a list, when the items are longer than one or two words each:

> **This is what went wrong on holiday: the flight was late; the hotel was dirty; the food was horrible; it rained every day; and I ended up with an ear infection.**

> **Here is the fireworks code: keep fireworks in a closed box; follow the instructions on each firework; light all fireworks at arm's length; stand well back; never go back to a lit firework; never put fireworks in your pocket; never throw fireworks; and keep pets indoors.**

- To mark a break in a sentence, especially when you are showing a contrast or balance between two things:

> **Jack loves football; his brother hates it.**

> **The wedding is in July; the weather should be warm then.**

> **My family don't eat turkey at Christmas; we like to go for a curry instead.**

55

# Colon

The colon is a mark that looks like **:** (a full stop directly above another full stop). When you are writing a colon, the bottom full stop should sit just on top of the line.

## When should you use a colon in your writing?

- To introduce a list:

> The Jamaican flag contains three colours: black, green and gold.

> I need to get some things at the supermarket:
> tea, bread, apples, milk and cheese.

- To introduce a reason for something:

> We never go abroad on holiday: my father is scared of flying.

> You need to take a waterproof jacket: it's going to rain later.

# Hyphen

A hyphen is a mark that looks like a short line **-** which you put between words to join them together. When you are writing a hyphen, you put it above the line, about halfway between the top and the bottom of the letters you are joining.

## When should you use a hyphen in your writing?

Often, when you join words together, you do not need a hyphen because the words can just be put together to make a new word:

 **web + site = website**

But there are times when you need to put a hyphen between the words:

- To avoid having two vowels next to each other:

| pro-independence | re-elect | anti-ageing |

- To avoid confusion about how the word should be said:

  no-nonsense      mis-sell      pro-am

- To avoid confusion with another word:

  re-creation (recreation)    re-cover (recover)    re-count (recount)

- You also use a hyphen to avoid confusion about what a phrase means:

  hoodie wearing boys   hoodie-wearing boys (boys wearing hoodies)

  fish eating seabirds   fish-eating seabirds (seabirds eating fish)

  flag waving fans   flag-waving fans (fans waving flags)

# Bullet point

A bullet point is a mark that comes before an item in a list. It is usually in the shape of a large solid dot • and you put it halfway between the top and bottom of the word that follows it.

## When should you use bullet points in your writing?

You use bullet points when you are making points in a list:

Games for a child's birthday party:

- musical chairs
- pass the parcel
- pin the tail on the donkey
- memory tray
- musical statues

You put a colon after the introduction to the list. The items in the list should all start with a small letter, unless they are full sentences, and then they start with a capital letter and have a full stop afterwards.

**Ellipsis**

# Ellipsis

The ellipsis is a mark made up of three full stops ... and it is used to show that part of the sentence is missing.

## When should you use the ellipsis in your writing?

- You use the ellipsis to show that some words are missing. You would insert an ellipsis if you were using a long quotation from someone and you did not want to include the whole quotation. By using an ellipsis you can leave out the words that you do not need, but you can make it clear that the quotation is not being written exactly. This is important when you write reports .

Here is a quotation from a very famous speech:

> "I have a dream that one day even the state of Mississippi, a state sweltering with the heat of injustice, sweltering with the heat of oppression, will be transformed into an oasis of freedom and justice."
> Martin Luther King Jr

Here it is in a shorter form with ellipsis:

> "I have a dream that one day even the state of Mississippi ... will be transformed into an oasis of freedom and justice."

- Ellipsis is also used when you want to show a pause in a character's speech:

"Why are you late?" demanded the head teacher.

"Well ... I ... I'm not sure," muttered the boy.

- Ellipsis can also help us to create a dramatic ending to a story:

Two red eyes appeared in the cave ...

# Spelling

## The alphabet

The English alphabet has 26 letters:

### a b c d e f g h i j k l m n o p q r s t u v w x y z

Letters are sorted into two groups, consonants and vowels. They are separated like this because you make a different sound when you say them.

## Consonants

Twenty letters in the alphabet are called consonants:

### b c d f g h j k l m n p q r s t v w x z

When you make a consonant sound, you stop the sound with your lips, tongue or teeth. For example, when you make the sound /f/, you put your bottom lip against your top teeth. When the air passes between them, it makes the /f/ sound.

## Vowels

Five of the letters are called vowels:

### a e i o u

A vowel sound is one which is produced without the air being stopped in any way.

## The letter y

The letter **y** is special. It can be a vowel or a consonant.

| party   style | = vowel |
| --- | --- |
| yellow   backyard | = consonant |

It is most often grouped with the consonants.

# Syllables

A syllable is one part of a word with one vowel sound which is said as a single unit or beat.

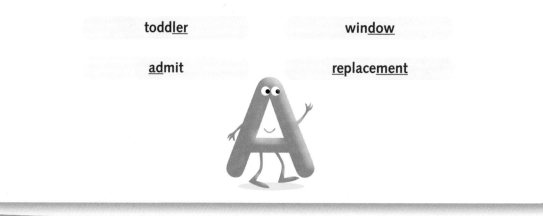

Here are some words with one syllable:

| man | house | friend | shore |

Here are some words with two syllables:

| woman | palace | husband | teacher |

Here are some words with three syllables:

| overtake | compliment | riverside | telephone |

## Stressed syllables

When you say a word with more than one syllable, you do not put the same emphasis – or stress – on each syllable. You say some syllables more strongly than others. These are the stressed syllables. Look at the parts of the words that are underlined below:

toddler        window        admit        replacement

## Unstressed syllables

Syllables without this stress are called unstressed syllables. These parts are underlined below:

toddler        window

admit        replacement

# Letters and sounds

When spelling, it is important to understand the difference between the way we say a sound and the way we write it.

## Phonemes

A phoneme is the smallest unit of sound we can make that is different from other sounds. We write the phoneme sounds between slashes:

*din*          /d/ + /i/ + /n/

There are about 44 phonemes in English, depending on the accent you have.

## Graphemes

A grapheme is the letter or combination of letters used to write a phoneme:

| Phoneme | Grapheme |
|---------|----------|
| /m/ | **m** (as in *room*) |
| /f/ | **f** (as in *fin*)   **ph** (as in *photo*) |
| /t/ | **t** (as in *cat*)   **tt** (as in *kitten*)   **ght** (as in *fight*) |

# Consonants and their phonemes and graphemes

**b**  The phoneme /b/ is written as **b** or **bb**, as in *bake* and *rubbing.*

**d**  The phoneme /d/ is written as **d**, **dd** or **ed**, as in *dog, rudder* and *pulled.*

**f**  The phoneme /f/ is written as **f**, **ff**, **gh** or **ph**, as in *face, scoff, laugh* and *photo.*
It is usually spelt as **ff** if it comes straight after a single vowel in a short word, like *cliff.*
But watch out for: *if*
It is usually spelt as **f** in short everyday words, like *fun, fit, fall, full* and *finish.*

**g**  The phoneme /g/ is written as **g** or **gg**, as in *gate* and *bigger.*
In some words ending in the /g/ sound, it is spelt **gue**, as in *league* and *plague.*

**h**  The phoneme /h/ is written as **h**, as in *help.*

**k**  The phoneme /k/ is written as **c**, **ck**, **k**, **ch** or **qu**, as in *cat, luck, kite, school* and *mosquito.*
It is usually spelt as **ck** if it comes straight after a single vowel in a short word, like *back.*
It is spelt as **k** if it comes before **e**, **i** and **y**, as in *sketch, skin, kit* and *risky.*
It is spelt as **ch** in some words which originally came from Greek, like *scheme, chorus* and *echo.*
In some words ending in the /k/ sound, it is spelt **que**, as in *antique* and *unique.*
The /kw/ sound at the beginning of a word is spelt **qu**, as in *queen, quick, quit* and *question.*

**l**  The phoneme /l/ is written as **l** or **ll**, as in *life* and *doll.*
It is usually spelt as **ll** if it comes straight after a short vowel sound, like *hill* or *villain.*
But watch out for: *pal*

**m**  The phoneme /m/ is written as **m**, **mm**, **mn** or **mb**, as in *mouse, summer, autumn* and *lamb.*

**n**  The phoneme /n/ is written as **n**, **nn**, **gn**, **kn**, **mn** or **pn**, as in *net, dinner, gnome, knife, mnemonic* and *pneumonia*.
When a word starts with **kn**, you do not say the **k**, as in *knight* and *knee*.
When a word starts with **gn**, you do not say the **g**, as in *gnaw*.
When a word starts with **mn** or **pn**, you do not say the **m** or **p**, as in *mnemonic* and *pneumatic*.

**p**  The phoneme /p/ is written as **p** or **pp**, as in *pond* and *supper*.

**r**  The phoneme /r/ is written as **r**, **rr**, **wr** or **rh**, as in *rude, sorry, write* and *rhyme*.
When a word starts with **wr**, you do not say the **w**, as in *wrong*.

**s**  The phoneme /s/ is written as **s**, **ss**, **c**, **sc**, **ps** or **st**, as in *silver, messy, cellar, science, psychiatry* and *listen*.
It is usually spelt as **ss** if it comes straight after a single vowel in a short word, like *kiss*.
But watch out for: *bus, yes, us*
It is spelt as **c** before **e**, **i** and **y**, as in *face, rice, centre, civil* and *mercy*.
It is spelt as **sc** in some words which originally came from Latin, like *scenery, descent* and *discipline*.

**t**  The phoneme /t/ is written as **t**, **tt**, **ght**, **ed**, **th** or **bt**, as in *top, letter, height, jumped, Thomas* and *doubt*.

**v**  The phoneme /v/ is written as **v** or **vv**, as in *victory* and *skivvy*.
If a word ends with the /v/ phoneme, it is usually spelt **ve**, as in *have, live* and *give*.
English words almost never end with the letter **v**.
But watch out for: *of*

**w**  The phoneme /w/ is written as **w** or **wh**, as in *wild* and *which*.

**z**  The phoneme /z/ is written as **z**, **zz**, **s**, **se** or **ze**, as in *zoo, fizzy, homes, please* and *breeze*.
It is usually spelt as **zz** if it comes straight after a single vowel in a short word, like *jazz*.

**ð**  The phoneme /ð/ is written as **th**, as in *that* and *brother*.

**θ**  The phoneme /θ/ is written as **th**, as in *think* and *tooth*.

**Consonants**

 **dʒ** The phoneme /dʒ/ is written as **g**, **j** or **dge**, as in *general*, *jump* and *badger*.
The letter **j** is never used for the /dʒ/ sound at the end of words.
The /dʒ/ phoneme at the end of a word is spelt as **dge** if it comes after /æ/, /ɛ/, /ɪ/, /ɒ/ and /ʌ/, as in *badge*, *hedge*, *ridge*, *lodge* and *nudge*.
After all other sounds, if /dʒ/ is at the end of a word, it is spelt as **ge**, as in *wage*, *huge*, *barge*, *range*, *bulge* and *village*.
Elsewhere in words, /dʒ/ is spelt as **j** before **a**, **o** and **u**, as in *jam*, *jotter*, *junk* and *adjust*.
It is often spelt as **g** before **e**, **i** and **y**, as in *gem*, *ginger*, *giraffe* and *energy*.
But watch out for: *jelly*, *jewel*, *jet*, *jig*, *jinx*

**j** The phoneme /j/ is written as **y**, as in *young*.

**ŋ** The phoneme /ŋ/ is written as **ng**, as in *ring* and *singer*.
It is written as **n** when it comes before **k**, as in *think*, *blank*, *chunk* and *honk*.

**ʃ** The phoneme /ʃ/ is written as **sh**, **ch** or **s**, as in *ship*, *chef* and *sugar*.
It is spelt as **ch** in some words which originally came from French, like *chalet*, *machine* and *brochure*.

**tʃ** The phoneme /tʃ/ is written as **ch** or **tch**, as in *chocolate* and *witch*.
It is usually spelt as **tch** if it comes straight after a single vowel, as in *fetch* and *catch*.
But watch out for: *rich*, *which*, *much*, *such*

**ʒ** The phoneme /ʒ/ is written as **s** or **z**, as in *measure* and *azure*.

**x** The letter X represents the sound /ks/ or /gz/, as in *box* and *exam*.

## Vowels and their phonemes and graphemes

**ɑː** The phoneme /ɑː/ is written as **a**, as in *father*.

**ɒ** The phoneme /ɒ/ is written as **o**, as in *lot*.
When it comes after **w** or **qu**, it is spelt as **a**, as in *want, watch, quality* and *squash*.

**æ** The phoneme /æ/ is written as **a**, as in *hat*.

**aɪ** The phoneme /aɪ/ is written as **i**, **i_e**, **ie** or **igh**, as in *blind, time, lie* and *sigh*.
When it comes at the end of a word, it is usually spelt as **y**, as in *cry, dry, apply* and *July*.

**aʊ** The phoneme /aʊ/ is written as **ou** or **ow**, as in *pound* and *down*.

**ɛ** The phoneme /ɛ/ is written as **e** or **ea**, as in *bed* and *head*.

**eɪ** The phoneme /eɪ/ is written as **ay**, **a_e** or **ai**, as in *play, date* and *faint*.
It can also be spelt as **ei**, as in *rein, vein* and *reindeer*.
It can be spelt as **eigh**, as in *eight, weigh* and *weight*.
It can be spelt as **ey**, as in *they, obey* and *prey*.
It can be spelt as **aigh**, as in *straight*.

**ɛə** The phoneme /ɛə/ is written as **air**, **are** or **ear** as in *fair, care* and *bear*.

**əʊ** The phoneme /əʊ/ is written as **o**, **oa**, **o_e** or **ow**, as in *hold, toad, bone* and *show*.

**ɪ** The phoneme /ɪ/ is written as **i**, as in *sing*.
When it comes at the end of a word, it is spelt as **y**, as in *very, silly, rugby* and *family*.
It can also be spelt **ey** at the end of a word, as in *valley, chimney* and *monkey*.
There are a few words where the phoneme is spelt as **y** when it does not come at the end: *gym, myth, pyramid, mystery, Egypt*

**ɪə** The phoneme /ɪə/ is written as **eer**, **ear**, **ere** or **ier**, as in *jeer, hear, here* and *pier*.

**iː** The phoneme /iː/ is written as **e**, **ea**, **ee**, **e_e** or **ie**, as in *he, steal, tree, theme* and *thief*.
It can also be spelt **ey** when it is at the end of a word, as in *key*.
When it comes after **c**, it is spelt as **ei**, as in *deceive, receive, ceiling* and *conceit*.

**ɔː** The phoneme /ɔː/ is written as **au**, **aw** or **or**, as in *cause, dawn* and *corn*.
When it comes after **w**, it is spelt as **ar**, as in *war, warm, wart* and *towards*.
When it comes before **l** or **ll**, it is spelt as **a**, as in *walk, always, ball* and *fall*.

**ɔɪ** The phoneme /ɔɪ/ is written as **oi** or **oy**, as in *join* and *toy*.

**ʊ** The phoneme /ʊ/ is written as **oo** or **ou**, as in *look* and *could*.

**ʊə** The phoneme /ʊə/ is written as **our**, **ure** or **oor**, as in *tour, sure* and *poor*.

**uː** The phoneme /uː/ is written as **oo**, **ou**, **ue** or **u_e**, as in *boot, you, true* and *flute*.

**ʌ** The phoneme /ʌ/ is written as **u**, as in *mug*.
It can be spelt as **o**, as in *other, son, nothing* and *Monday*.
It is spelt as **ou** in a few words: *young, touch, trouble, double* and *country*.

**ɜː** The phoneme /ɜː/ is written as **er**, **ur** or **ir**, as in *herd, burn* and *third*.
When it comes after **w**, it is spelt as **or**.
There are not many of these words:
*word, worm, world, work, worth, worse, worst*

**ə** The phoneme /ə/ is written as **er**, as in *father*.

# Digraphs and trigraphs

A digraph is a grapheme where two letters represent one phoneme:

| grapheme | phoneme | example |
|----------|---------|---------|
| **ea** | /iː/ | *seat* |
| **sh** | /ʃ/ | *shoot* |

A split diagraph is when the two letters in a digraph are separated by another letter:

| split digraph | phoneme | example |
|---------------|---------|---------|
| **u_e** | /uː/ | *crude* |
| **i_e** | /aɪ/ | *slime* |

A trigraph is a grapheme where three letters represent one phoneme:

| trigraph | phoneme | example |
|----------|---------|---------|
| **tch** | /tʃ/ | *watch* |
| **igh** | /aɪ/ | *light* |

## Vowel digraphs and trigraphs

Here are the digraphs and trigraphs that represent English vowel sounds.

**a_e**  as in  *take, same, made, grape*

**ai**  as in  *rain, pain, afraid, wait*
This is never used at the end of a word.

**air**  as in  *air, stairs, chair, fairy*

**ar**  as in  *bar, dark, harm, garden*

**are**  as in  *stare, care, scared, compare*

**au**  as in  *author, audience, thesaurus, dinosaur*

Digraphs and trigraphs

**aw**    as in    *saw, awful, lawn, crawl*

**ay**    as in    *day, stay, play, waylay*
This is used at the end of a word and the end of a syllable.

**ea**    as in    *sea, lean, reach, meat*
       as in    *head, bread, instead, meant*
       as in    *great, break, steak*

**ear**    as in    *clear, year, beard, appear*
       as in    *bear, wear, pear*

**ee**    as in    *see, meet, peek, agree*

**e_e**    as in    *these, extreme, theme, concrete*

**er**    as in    *her, term, verb, person*
       as in    *clever, over, mother, gather*

**ew**    as in    *new, few, grew, drew*
This digraph can be used for 'oo' sounds like *drew* and 'yoo' sounds like *new*.

**ie**    as in    *die, tried, lie, pie*
       as in    *chief, field, relief, thief*

**i_e**    as in    *hide, bike, kite, time, alive*

**igh**    as in    *fright, high, sigh, night*

**ir**    as in    *girl, bird, skirt, first*

**oa**    as in    *goal, boat, road, goat*
There are very few words that end in **oa**.

**oe**    as in    *toe, goes, woe*
       as in    *shoe*

**o_e**    as in    *rope, mole, those, joke*

# Spelling

**oi**  as in  *oil, join, point, toil*
This is almost never used at the end of a word.

**oo**  as in  *wood, fool, moon, food*
as in  *book, took, foot, wood, good*
Very few words end in **oo**.
But watch out for:  *zoo, shampoo, igloo*

**or**  as in  *for, short, horse, form*

**ore**  as in  *wore, swore, before, more*

**ou**  as in  *out, round, south, loud*
as in  *could, would, should*
There are very few words that end in **ou**.
But watch out for:  *you*

**ow**  as in  *town, crowd, now, frown*
as in  *own, grow, blow, snow*

**oy**  as in  *toy, boy, enjoy, royal*
This is mostly used at the end of a word and the end of a syllable.

**ue**  as in  *blue, clue, true, rescue*
This digraph can be used for 'oo' sounds like *blue* and 'yoo' sounds
like *rescue*.

**u_e**  as in  *use, rule, tune, rude*
This digraph can be used for 'oo' sounds like *rule* and 'yoo' sounds
like *use*.

**ur**  as in  *burn, turn, hurt, Thursday*

# Adding endings to words

Adding endings to root words can change their meanings. There are some rules to help you know how to spell the new words you make.

## Making nouns plural

One person or thing is called the singular, for example **one elephant**. More than one is called the plural, for example **two elephants**. When you make a singular noun plural, you change it by adding the ending (or suffix) **-s** or **-es**. To work out whether to add **-s** or **-es**, look at the last letter or letters in the root word. That will show you how to make the plural.

### Adding -s

The simplest way to make a plural is to add **-s** to the end of the root word. This is how most nouns work.

| Last letter or letters | Root word | Plural |
|:---:|:---:|:---:|
| a | umbrella | umbrellas |
| b | job | jobs |
| c | attic | attics |
| d | word | words |
| e | tree | trees |
| ff | cliff | cliffs |
| g | log | logs |
| i | bikini | bikinis |
| k | stick | sticks |
| l | wall | walls |
| m | pram | prams |
| n | bin | bins |
| p | lamp | lamps |
| r | colour | colours |
| t | rat | rats |
| w | pillow | pillows |

# Spelling

## Adding -es

Some plurals are made by adding **-es**. Remember to look at the last letter or letters in the root word.

| Last letter or letters | Root word | Plural |
|:---:|:---:|:---:|
| ch | wit**ch** | witches |
| sh | wi**sh** | wishes |
| s | bu**s** | buses |
| ss | ki**ss** | kisses |
| x | fo**x** | foxes |
| z | bu**zz** | buzzes |

## Nouns that end in f or fe

When a word ends in **f**, change the **f** to **v** and add **-es**:

thief→ thieves      leaf → leaves      half → halves      loaf → loaves

When a word ends in **fe**, change the **fe** to **ve** and add **-s**:

life → lives      knife → knives

## Nouns that end in o

For most nouns that end in **o**, make the plural by adding **-s**:

piano → pianos      shampoo → shampoos      zero → zeros

But watch out for a few that add **-es** instead:

echo → echoes      tomato → tomatoes

potato → potatoes      hero → heroes

## Nouns that end in y

If the last letter of a noun is **y**, look at the letter before the **y** to know how to make it a plural. If the letter before the **y** is a vowel, add **-s**:

day → days          key → keys          toy → toys          guy → guys

If the letter before the **y** is a consonant, change the **y** to **i** and then add **-es**:

fairy → fairies     quality → qualities     spy → spies     mummy → mummies

## But ...

There are some exceptions to the rules about making nouns plural.

child → children     man → men     woman → women     mouse → mice

tooth → teeth     goose → geese     ox → oxen     person → people

## And ...

Some words are the same for the singular and plural.

sheep → sheep     deer → deer     pence → pence     fish → fish

# Comparing adjectives

The comparative of an adjective means 'more' and to make it add **-er** to the end. The superlative means 'most' and you make it by adding **-est**.

small          smaller          smallest

## Adding -er and -est without change

For most adjectives of one or two syllables, add **-er** or **-est** without making any other change to the word:

high          higher          highest

dark          darker          darkest

quiet          quieter          quietest

## Adjectives ending in y

If the last letter is **y** and the letter before it is a consonant, change the **y** to **i** and add **-er** or **-est**:

| | | |
|---|---|---|
| happy | happier | happiest |
| silly | sillier | silliest |
| merry | merrier | merriest |

## Adjectives ending in e

If the last letter is **e**, drop the **e** and add **-er** or **-est**:

| | | |
|---|---|---|
| nice | nicer | nicest |
| tame | tamer | tamest |
| rare | rarer | rarest |

## Some adjectives with one syllable

If an adjective has one syllable and ends with a single vowel followed by a single consonant, double the consonant and add **-er** or **-est**:

| | | |
|---|---|---|
| fat | fatter | fattest |
| sad | sadder | saddest |
| slim | slimmer | slimmest |

# Inflecting verbs

Verbs can be written in different ways. These are called inflections. There are verb inflections for four different things: third person singular present tense, present participle, past tense and past participle.

## Third person singular present tense

This form of verb is used when talking about one person or thing doing something now. To make it add **-s** or **-es** to the end of verb:

walk → walks   Jack walks to school.

catch → catches   The dog catches the ball in its mouth.

### Adding -s

For most verbs, just add **-s**:

climb → climbs        trace → traces        remember → remembers

### Adding -es

If a verb ends in **ch**, **sh**, **ss**, **x** or **z**, add **-es**:

pinch → pinches        push → pushes        pass → passes

box → boxes                    fizz → fizzes

### Verbs ending in y

If the verb ends in **y** and the letter before it is a consonant, change the **y** to **i** and add **-es**:

try → tries        reply → replies        copy → copies

If the verb ends in **y** and the letter before it is a vowel, you just add **-s**:

play → plays        key → keys        annoy → annoys

## Present participle

This form of the verb ends in **-ing**.
It is the one you use for the progressive present tense and the progressive past tense.

# Spelling

## Adding -ing

For most verbs, just add **-ing**:

read → reading     catch → catching     repeat → repeating     fly → flying

## Verbs ending in e

If the verb ends in **e**, drop the **e** and then add **-ing**:

like → liking          fade → fading          write → writing

## Some verbs with one syllable

If a verb has one syllable and ends a single vowel followed by a single consonant, double the consonant and add **-ing**:

hit → hitting          bat → batting          hum → humming

But watch out for:

boxing          fixing          mixing

## Verbs ending in ie

There is a small group of verbs that end in **ie**:

die          lie          tie          untie          vie

For these you replace the **ie** with **y** before adding **-ing**:

dying          lying          tying          untying          vying

## Verbs ending in fer

If the verb ends in **fer**, you double the final **r** before adding **-ing**:

refer → referring     transfer → transferring     prefer → preferring

## Verbs with more than one syllable

This rule is for verbs that have more than one syllable and end in a single vowel followed by a single consonant. If the final syllable is stressed, double the consonant and then add **-ing**:

admit → admitting    equip → equipping    regret → regretting

If the final syllable is not stressed, you just add **-ing**:

limit → limiting    listen → listening    order → ordering

## Past tense

The past tense is the form used to describe an action that has already happened. To make this add **-ed** or **-d**.

### Adding -ed

For most verbs, just add **-ed**:

rain → rained    design → designed    clear → cleared

### Verbs ending in e

If a verb ends in **e**, add **-d**:

smile → smiled    like → liked    separate → separated

### Verbs ending in y

If the verb ends in **y** and the letter before it is a consonant, change the **y** to **i** and add **-ed**:

rely → relied    dry → dried    occupy → occupied

If the verb ends in **y** and the letter before it is a vowel, just add **-ed**:

replay → replayed    annoy → annoyed    key → keyed

## Some verbs with one syllable

If a verb has one syllable and ends a single vowel followed by a single consonant, double the consonant and add **-ed**:

hop → hopped        sin → sinned        spot → spotted

But watch out for:

boxed        fixed        mixed

## Verbs ending in fer

If the verb ends in **fer**, double the final **r** before adding **-ed**:

refer → referred        transfer → transferred        prefer → preferred

## Verbs with more than one syllable

This rule is for verbs that have more than one syllable and end in a single vowel followed by a single consonant. If the final syllable is stressed, double the consonant and then add **-ed**:

admit → admitted        equip → equipped        regret → regretted

If the final syllable is not stressed, just add **-ed**:

limit → limited        listen → listened        order → ordered

## Past participle

The past participle is the form of the verb that is used with the auxiliary verb **have** to make the present perfect tense or the past perfect tense. For most verbs, the past participle is the same as the past tense:

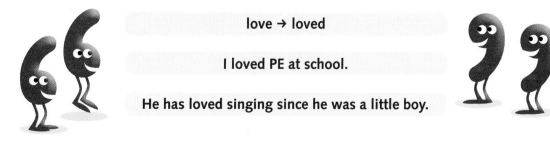

love → loved

I loved PE at school.

He has loved singing since he was a little boy.

# Irregular verbs

There are many commonly used verbs which have a different past tense and past participle. Here is a list of some of them.

| Verb | Past tense | Past participle |
|---|---|---|
| begin | began | begun |
| bite | bit | bitten |
| blow | blew | blown |
| break | broke | broken |
| choose | chose | chosen |
| draw | drew | drawn |
| drink | drank | drunk |
| drive | drove | driven |
| eat | ate | eaten |
| fall | fell | fallen |
| fly | flew | flown |
| forget | forgot | forgotten |
| forgive | forgave | forgiven |
| freeze | froze | frozen |
| give | gave | given |
| grow | grew | grown |
| know | knew | known |
| lie | lay | lain |
| ride | rode | ridden |
| ring | rang | rung |
| rise | rose | risen |
| run | ran | run |
| see | saw | seen |
| swear | swore | sworn |
| swim | swam | swum |
| shake | shook | shaken |

| Verb | Past tense | Past participle |
|------|-----------|-----------------|
| sing | sang | sung |
| sink | sank | sunk |
| speak | spoke | spoken |
| steal | stole | stolen |
| take | took | taken |
| tear | tore | torn |
| throw | threw | thrown |
| wake | woke | woken |
| wear | wore | worn |
| write | wrote | written |

## Other irregular verbs

Here are some other verbs which do not follow the rules for inflections.
These verbs (and the ones in the previous list) are known as irregular verbs.

| Verb | Past tense | Past participle |
|------|-----------|-----------------|
| beat | beat | beaten |
| become | became | become |
| bend | bent | bent |
| bring | brought | brought |
| build | built | built |
| burst | burst | burst |
| buy | bought | bought |
| catch | caught | caught |
| come | came | come |
| cost | cost | cost |
| cut | cut | cut |
| feed | fed | fed |
| feel | felt | felt |
| fight | fought | fought |

| Verb | Past tense | Past participle |
| --- | --- | --- |
| find | found | found |
| get | got | got |
| hang | hung | hung |
| hear | heard | heard |
| hit | hit | hit |
| hold | held | held |
| keep | kept | kept |
| lead | led | led |
| leave | left | left |
| lend | lent | lent |
| light | lit | lit |
| make | made | made |
| mean | meant | meant |
| pay | paid | paid |
| put | put | put |
| sell | sold | sold |
| send | sent | sent |
| shoot | shot | shot |
| sit | sat | sat |
| sleep | slept | slept |
| slide | slid | slid |
| spend | spent | spent |
| stand | stood | stood |
| teach | taught | taught |
| tell | told | told |
| think | thought | thought |
| weep | wept | wept |
| win | won | won |

# Adding prefixes and suffixes

Sometimes you have to change the way a word is spelt when you add a prefix or a suffix to create a new word.

## Prefixes

In most cases you do not have to change the root word when you add a prefix to it. You can usually join the word and the prefix together without making any changes to either:

un- + successful = unsuccessful

dis- + obey = disobey

The exception to this is **in-**, which changes depending on the first letter of the root word. You can see more about this on page 28. You can read about the meanings of prefixes on pages 28–29.

## Suffixes

It is possible that you will have to change the spelling of the root word when you add a suffix. It depends on the last letter or letters of the root word, and the first letter of the suffix. You can read more about the meanings of suffixes on pages 30–32.

### Suffixes beginning with a consonant

If a suffix starts with a consonant, you can add it on to most root words without making any changes to the root word:

-ment    agree + -ment = agreement

-ness    gentle + -ness = gentleness

-ful    spite + -ful = spiteful

-less    fear + -less = fearless

But watch out for:    argument

Adding prefixes and suffixes

If the root word has more than one syllable and ends with a consonant followed by **y**, you change the **y** to **i** and then add the suffix:

merry → merriment

silly → silliness

plenty → plentiful

pity → pitiless

## The suffix -ly

This suffix turns an adjective into an adverb. It can be added straight to adjectives that end in a consonant:

stupid + -ly          stupidly

usual + -ly           usually

complete + -ly        completely

If the adjective has more than one syllable and ends with a consonant followed by **y**, you change the **y** to **i** and then add **-ly**:

happy → happily

angry → angrily

If the adjective ends in **le**, you change the **e** to **y**:

gentle → gently

simple → simply

If the adjective ends in **ic**, you add **-ally**:

dramatic → dramatically

basic → basically

But watch out for:

truly          duly          wholly

## Suffixes beginning with a vowel

In many cases you can add the suffix without changing the root word:

-able      agree + -able = agreeable

-ation      inform + -ation = information

-er      paint + -er = painter

-ance      perform + -ance = performance

-ence      correspond + -ence = correspondence

**Some root words with one syllable**

If a root word has one syllable and ends a single vowel followed by a single consonant, double the consonant and add the suffix:

drum → drummer      win → winnable      hug → huggable

## Words with more than one syllable

This rule is for root words that have more than one syllable and end in a single vowel followed by a single consonant. If the final syllable is stressed, double the consonant and then add the suffix:

admit → admittance      regret → regrettable

If the final syllable is not stressed, just add the suffix:

limit → limitation      listen → listener

## Root words ending in y

If the root word ends in **y** and the letter before it is a consonant, change the **y** to **i** and add the suffix:

deny → deniable      rely → reliance

If the root word ends in **y** and the letter before it is a vowel, just add the suffix:

play → playable                    annoy → annoyance

## Words ending in silent e

If the letter **e** at the end of a word is not pronounced, we say it is silent, as in **sense** and **live**.

When you add a suffix beginning with a vowel to a root word that ends in silent **e**, you drop the **e** before adding the suffix:

sense → sensible        adore → adorable      prepare → preparation

## Adding -able to words ending in ce or ge

You keep the silent **e** when you add **-able** to words that end in **ce** or **ge**:

notice → noticeable                    replace → replaceable

change → changeable                    manage → manageable

## Words ending in fer

If the **fer** part of the word is stressed when the suffix is added, double the **r** and then add the suffix:

refer → referral                    defer → deferral

If the **fer** part is not stressed when the suffix is added, just add the suffix:

prefer → preference                 transfer → transferable

## The suffix -ous

You can add this to some words without any change:

poison → poisonous                    cancer → cancerous

mountain → mountainous

# Spelling

## Words ending in silent e

If the root word ends in a silent **e**, drop the **e** before adding **-ous**:

fame → famous          carnivore → carnivorous

## Words ending in ge

If the root word ends in **ge** and you want to keep the /dʒ/ sound, just add the suffix:

courage → courageous          outrage → outrageous

## Words ending in y

If the root word ends in **y**, change the **y** to **i** and add **-ous**:

glory → glorious          fury → furious          harmony → harmonious

But watch out for:          **joyous**

## Words ending in our

If the root word ends in **our**, change it to **or** and then add **-ous**:

humour → humorous          odour → odorous          glamour → glamorous

## Adding the suffix -y

You can add **-y** to many words without any change:

rain → rainy          yellow → yellowy          salt → salty

If the root word ends in **e**, drop the e and add **-y**:

whine → whiny          spike → spiky          bone → bony

If the root word has one syllable and ends in a single vowel followed by a single consonant, double the final consonant and then add **-y**:

sun → sunny          fad → faddy          drip → drippy

But watch out for:

boxy          foxy          waxy          sexy

# Common endings in words

Some endings often appear in English words.
Certain sounds can also be spelt in more than one way.

## Words ending in /l/ or /əl/ sound

These are most often spelt with **le**:

| table | middle | bottle | fiddle |

When it comes after **m, n, r, s, v** and **w**, it is spelt **el**:

| camel | tunnel | squirrel | travel |

It is usually spelt **el** when it comes after **s**:

| tinsel | chisel | vessel | easel |

Not many words end in **il**:

| pencil | council | stencil | fossil |

| tonsil | April | nostril | peril |

Many adjectives end in **al**:

| medical | radical | normal | additional |

Not many nouns end in **al**:

| medal | metal | pedal | capital | animal | hospital |

## Words ending in /ʃən/ sound

The most common spelling is **tion**:

| station | relation | action | adoption |

It is used when the root word ends in **t** or **te**.

If the root word ends in **ss** or **mit**, the spelling is **ssion**:

admission          recession          expression          omission

If the root word ends in **d**, **de** or **se**, the spelling is **sion**:

extension          erosion          comprehension          tension

But watch out for:

attend → attention                    intend → intention

If the root word ends in **c** or **cs**, the spelling is **cian**:

musician          electrician          politician          optician

# Words ending in /ʒən/ sound

This sound is spelt **sion**:

division          invasion          vision          conclusion

# Words ending in /ʒə/ sound

This is always spelt **sure**:

measure          pleasure          leisure          composure

# Words ending in /tʃe/ sound

This is often spelt **ture**:

adventure          fracture          lecture          nature

It can sometimes be spelt **cher** or **tcher**:

teacher          researcher          butcher          catcher

## Words ending in /ʃəs/ sound

Some of these are spelt **cious**:

| | | | |
|---|---|---|---|
| vicious | delicious | ferocious | suspicious |

Others are spelt **tious**:

| | | | |
|---|---|---|---|
| cautious | ambitious | repetitious | fictitious |

But watch out for:   **anxious**

## Words ending in /ɪəs/ sound

These are most often spelt **ious**:

| | | | |
|---|---|---|---|
| hilarious | glorious | serious | mysterious |

Some are spelt **eous**:

| | | | | |
|---|---|---|---|---|
| courteous | spontaneous | simultaneous | hideous | nauseous |

## Words ending in /ʃəl/ sound

After a vowel this is usually spelt **cial**:

| | | | |
|---|---|---|---|
| racial | social | special | official |

After a consonant this is usually spelt **tial**:

| | | | |
|---|---|---|---|
| essential | partial | potential | substantial |

But watch out for:

| | | | |
|---|---|---|---|
| initial | provincial | financial | commercial |

# Choosing between endings

> Sometimes you have to choose between endings that sound the same or similar.

## Is it ant or ent?

If there is a related word ending in **ation**, use **ant**:

> tolerant (toleratation)   dominant (domination)   stagnant (stagnation)

This is also true for **ance** and **ancy**:

> dominance (domination)                hesitancy (hesitation)

You use **ent** if it comes after **c** when it sounds like /s/, after **g** when it sounds like /dʒ/, or after the letters **qu**:

> recent                agent                frequent

This is also true for **ence** and **ency**:

> innocence            intelligence            sequence
>
> decency              emergency              delinquency

But watch out for:

> assistant            obedient            independent

## Is it able or ible?

There are far more words ending in **able** than **ible**.

If there is a related word that ends in **ation**, use **able**:

> admirable (admiration)                abominable (abomination)
>
> considerable (consideration)

If an adjective ends in **able**, its adverb ends in **ably**:

> admirably            abominably            considerably

A word usually ends in **able** if, when you say it without the ending, the first part of the word sounds like a complete root word:

> **affordable = afford + able**

> **fashionable = fashion + able**

> **reliable = reli + able (reli sounds like rely)**

If you do this and the first part of the word does not sound like a complete root word, the ending is likely to be **ible**:

> **edible = ed + ible**

> **possible = poss + ible**

> **invisible = invis + ible**

But watch out for:     **sensible**

If an adjective ends in **ible**, its adverb ends in **ibly**:

**horribly**          **impossibly**          **irresistibly**

# Words ending in ough

This is one of the strangest spellings in the English language. It can be pronounced more ways than any other group of letters. You have to learn these words one by one:

/ɔː/    **bought, ought, thought, brought, fought, nought**

/ʌf/    **rough, tough, enough**

/ɒf/    **cough**

/əʊ/    **though**

/uː/    **through**

/ə/    **thorough**

/aʊ/    **plough, bough**

# Silent letters

English has a number of silent letters. A silent letter is one that you do not pronounce when you say the word out loud. You have to learn most of these word by word.

silent **b** before **t**:   debt   doubt

silent **b** after **m**:   climb   dumb   numb   lamb   comb   thumb   bomb   womb

silent **c** after **s**:   science   scissors   scene   descent   muscle

silent **d**:   handsome   handkerchief   sandwich

final silent **e**:   love   hate   replace   tune   admire   complete   recede

silent **g** before **n**:   gnome   gnarled   gnat   gnaw   sign   foreign   reign

silent **h** after **g**:   ghost   ghastly   ghetto   gherkin

silent **h** after **w**:   when   wheat   whale   why   what   who   which

(People with Scottish accents pronounce the **h** after **w**)

silent **h** after **r**:   rhyme   rhythm   rhino   rhombus   rhubarb   rheumatism

silent **h** after **c**:   chemical   chaos   character   choir   chorus   Christmas

silent **h** at the beginning of a word:   hour   honest   honour   heir

silent **k** before **n**:   knight   knee   knife   know   knit   knock   kneel

silent **l** between **a** and **k**:   talk   stalk   walk   chalk

silent **l** between **a** and **m**:   calm   palm   qualm   balm   psalm   salmon   almond

silent **l** between **o** and **k**:   folk   yolk

silent **l** between **a** and **f**:   calf   half   behalf

silent **l** after **ou**:   could   should   would

silent **n** after **m**:   autumn   column   condemn   hymn   solemn   damn

silent **p** before **n**:   pneumonia   pneumatic

silent **p** before **s**:   psalm   psychiatry   psychopath   psychology

silent **s**:   island   isle   aisle   debris

silent **t**:   listen   whistle   thistle   fasten   Christmas   mortgage

silent **w** before **r**:   write   wrong   wreck   wrap   wrinkle   wrist

other words with a silent **w**:   two   sword   answer

## Some very common words that you have to know

A lot of words that we use all the time do not follow any of the normal rules of spelling.

| | | | |
|---|---|---|---|
| a | every | many | said |
| an | everybody | me | says |
| after | eye | mind | school |
| again | fast | money | she |
| any | father | most | should |
| are | find | move | so |
| ask | floor | Mr | some |
| bath | friend | Mrs | steak |
| be | full | my | sugar |
| beautiful | go | no | sure |
| because | gold | of | the |
| behind | grass | old | there |
| both | great | one | they |
| break | half | once | to |
| busy | has | only | today |
| by | he | our | told |
| child | her | pass | was |
| children | here | parents | water |
| Christmas | his | past | we |
| class | hold | path | were |
| climb | hour | people | where |
| clothes | house | plant | who |
| cold | I | poor | whole |
| come | improve | pretty | wild |
| could | is | prove | would |
| do | kind | pull | you |
| door | last | push | your |
| even | love | put | |

## Homophones

A homophone is a word that sounds the same as another word when you say it. There are a lot of these in English and they can be tricky to sort out.

| | | | |
|---|---|---|---|
| see | sea | meat | meet |
| bare | bear | missced | mist |
| one | won | peace | piece |
| son | sun | plain | plane |
| be | bee | rain   rein | reign |
| blue | blew | scene | seen |
| night | knight | weather | whether |
| brake | break | cereal | serial |
| fair | fare | past | passed |
| affect | effect | principle | principal |
| groan | grown | stationery | stationary |
| mail | male | steal | steel |

## It's and its

**It's** (with the apostrophe) is a short form of **it is** or **it has**.

**Its** (without the apostrophe) is a possessive pronoun that means 'belonging to it'.

> **It's** not my fault. (**It is** not my fault.)

> **It's** been ages since I saw you. (**It has** been ages since I saw you.)

> The horse fell during the race and broke **its** leg.

If you are not sure whether to use **it's** or **its**, try this. If you replace it in your sentence with **it is** or **it has**, does the sentence still make sense?

| | |
|---|---|
| I think **it's** time to go home. | I think **it is** time to go home. |
| My football has lost **its** bounce. | NOT My football has lost **it is** bounce. |

## There, their and they're

**There** is an adverb that tells you about where something is or where it happens.

**Their** is a possessive pronoun that means 'belonging to them'.

**They're** is a short form of **they are**.

She was standing over <u>there</u>.

The girls went back for <u>their</u> jackets.

If the children don't hurry up <u>they're</u> going to be late.

## To, too and two

**To** is a preposition that tells you about movement.

**Too** is an adverb that means 'as well'.

**Two** is the number between one and three.

We are going <u>to</u> the park.

Mary is coming <u>too</u>.

I have <u>two</u> pounds to spend.

# How to improve your spelling

There are a lot of things you can do to help you with your spelling.
The rules in this book will help you learn about making plurals,
inflecting verbs, comparing adjectives and adding prefixes and suffixes.
But there are other things you can do as well.

## Check your work

Always read what you have written a few times to see if you can spot any mistakes.
If you are not sure how to spell something, check it in a dictionary.

## Break it into syllables

If you don't know how to spell a word, break it into syllables and do it one syllable
at a time. Sound the phonemes out in your head, or even out loud.

## Words within words

When you are reading, look for words contained inside other words, like **get** in
**vegetable**, **par** in **separate** and **man** in **permanent**.

## Think about word families

If you are stuck on a word, try to think of other words that are in the same word
family, for example think about **irritate** if you are not sure how to spell **irritable**.

## Look, say, cover, write and check

Do this with any word you do not know:

- **Look** at it carefully.

- **Say** it out loud, listening to how it sounds.

- **Cover** the word and try to remember what it looks like.

- **Write** the word down.

- **Check** what you have written to see if it is right.

- Keep doing this until you can spell it without any mistakes.

# Mnemonics

A mnemonic is a way of remembering something. It is pronounced ni-**mon**-ik. They can help you remember difficult groups of letters or silent letters:

**big** **ea**rs **a**re **u**seful **t**o **y**ou = **beauty**

**big** **e**lephants **c**an **a**lways **u**nderstand **s**mall **e**lephants = **because**

There is **iron** in the environment = **environment**

My friend likes **fries** = **friend**

**Hide** those hideous things = **hideous**

**O**h **u** **l**ucky **d**uck = **should, could, would**

# How to use the Spelling Dictionary

You can see the first and last headwords on the page to help you find the page you need.

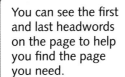

ability          **Dictionary**          aggressive

The headwords in the dictionary are in alphabetical order, making them easy to find.

## Aa

**ability** *noun* abilities
**absent** *adjective*
**absolute** *adjective*
**accent** *noun* accents
**accent** *verb* accents, accenting, accented
**accept** *verb* accepts, accepting, accepted

> Do not confuse the spellings of *accept* and *except*: *Please accept my apologies; He works every day except Tuesday*

**access** *verb* accesses, accessing, accessed
**accident** *noun* accidents
**accidentally\*** *adverb*
**accommodate\*** *verb* accommodates, accommodating, accommodated
**accommodation\*** *noun*
**accompany\*** *verb* accompanies, accompanying, accompanied
**according** *adjective*
**account** *noun* accounts
**account** *verb* accounts, accounting, accounted
**accountant\*** *noun* accountants
**ache** *noun* aches

**ache** *verb* aches, aching, ached
**achieve\*** *verb* achieves, achieving, achieved

> The *i* comes before the *e* in *achieve*

**achievement\*** *noun* achievements
**act** *noun* acts
**act** *verb* acts, acting, acted
**active** *adjective*
**activity** *noun* activities
**actor** *noun* actors
**actress** *noun* actresses
**actually** *adverb*
**ad** *noun* ads
**add** *verb* adds, adding, added
**address** *noun* addresses
**address** *verb* addresses, addressing, addressed
**adjective** *noun* adjectives
**admire** *verb* admires, admiring, admired
**admission** *noun* admissions
**admit** *verb* admits, admitting, admitted
**adult** *noun* adults
**advantage** *noun* advantages
**adventure** *noun* adventures
**adverb** *noun* adverbs
**advert** *noun* adverts

**advertise** *verb* advertises, advertising, advertised

> Some verbs can be spelt ending in either *ise* or *ize*, but *advertise* always has an *s*

**advertisement\*** *noun* advertisements
**advertiser** *noun* advertisers
**advice** *noun*

> The noun *advice* is spelt with a *c* and the verb *advise* is spelt with an *s*

**advise** *verb* advises, advising, advised
**aeroplane\*** *noun* aeroplanes
**affect** *verb* affects, affecting, affected

> Do not confuse the spelling of the verb *affect* with the noun *effect*. Something that *affects* you has an *effect* on you

**afford** *verb* affords, affording, afforded
**African** *noun* Africans
**afternoon** *noun* afternoons
**age** *noun* ages
**age** *verb* ages, ageing or aging, aged

> *Ageing* and *aging* are both correct spellings

**agency** *noun* agencies
**aggressive** *adjective*

You can see the word class of the headword, for example, noun, verb, adjective or adverb.

You can see other forms of the headword to help you spell it correctly with different endings.

Headwords which have a ✱ symbol are more difficult to spell.

Notes in green panels help you to avoid confusing the spelling of one word with another.

Notes in yellow panels give useful tips and information to help you spell the word correctly.

98

# Aa

**ability** *noun* abilities

**absent** *adjective*

**absolute** *adjective*

**accent** *noun* accents

**accent** *verb* accents, accenting, accented

**accept** *verb* accepts, accepting, accepted

Do not confuse the spellings of *accept* and *except*: Please accept my apologies; He works every day except Tuesday

**access** *verb* accesses, accessing, accessed

**accident** *noun* accidents

**accidentally\*** *adverb*

**accommodate\*** *verb* accommodates, accommodating, accommodated

**accommodation\*** *noun*

**accompany\*** *verb* accompanies, accompanying, accompanied

**according** *adjective*

**account** *noun* accounts

**account** *verb* accounts, accounting, accounted

**accountant\*** *noun* accountants

**ache** *noun* aches

**ache** *verb* aches, aching, ached

**achieve\*** *verb* achieves, achieving, achieved

The *i* comes before the *e* in *achieve*

**achievement\*** *noun* achievements

**act** *noun* acts

**act** *verb* acts, acting, acted

**active** *adjective*

**activity** *noun* activities

**actor** *noun* actors

**actress** *noun* actresses

**actually** *adverb*

**ad** *noun* ads

**add** *verb* adds, adding, added

**address** *noun* addresses

**address** *verb* addresses, addressing, addressed

**adjective** *noun* adjectives

**admire** *verb* admires, admiring, admired

**admission** *noun* admissions

**admit** *verb* admits, admitting, admitted

**adult** *noun* adults

**advantage** *noun* advantages

**adventure** *noun* adventures

**adverb** *noun* adverbs

**advert** *noun* adverts

**advertise** *verb* advertises, advertising, advertised

Some verbs can be spelt ending in either *ise* or *ize*, but *advertise* always has an *s*

**advertisement\*** *noun* advertisements

**advertiser** *noun* advertisers

**advice** *noun*

The noun *advice* is spelt with a *c* and the verb *advise* is spelt with an *s*

**advise** *verb* advises, advising, advised

**aeroplane\*** *noun* aeroplanes

**affect** *verb* affects, affecting, affected

Do not confuse the spelling of the verb *affect* with the noun *effect*. Something that *affects* you has an *effect* on you

**afford** *verb* affords, affording, afforded

**African** *noun* Africans

**afternoon** *noun* afternoons

**age** *noun* ages

**age** *verb* ages, ageing or aging, aged

*Ageing* and *aging* are both correct spellings

**agency** *noun* agencies

**aggressive** *adjective*

**agree** *verb* agrees, agreeing, agreed

**aim** *noun* aims

**aim** *verb* aims, aiming, aimed

**air** *noun* airs

**air** *verb* airs, airing, aired

**airline** *noun* airlines

**airport** *noun* airports

**alarm** *noun* alarms

**alarm** *verb* alarms, alarming, alarmed

**album** *noun* albums

**alcohol** *noun* alcohols

**alcoholic** *noun* alcoholics

**allow** *verb* allows, allowing, allowed

> Do not confuse the spellings of the past tense form *allowed* and the adverb *aloud*, which sound the same

**aloud** *adverb*

**alphabet** *noun* alphabets

**already** *adverb*

> Do not confuse the spellings of *already* and *all ready*. *Already* is an adverb. If something has *already* happened, it has happened before the present time: *I've already called an ambulance.* In the phrase **all ready**, *all* means the whole of a group or a thing, and *ready* is an adjective: *Are you all ready to go?*

**altar** *noun* altars

**alter** *verb* alters, altering, altered

> Do not confuse the spellings of *alter* and *altar*. *Alter* means to change something: *Nothing was altered today.* An *altar* is the holy table in a church: *The bishop stood in front of the altar*

**alternate** *adjective*

**alternate** *verb* alternates, alternating, alternated

> Do not confuse *alternate* and *alternative*. If something happens on *alternate* days, it happens on one day not on the next, then happens again the day after that: *She spends alternate weeks with her father.* You use *alternative* to describe something that can be used, had or done instead of something else: *I suggested an alternative route*

**alternative** *adjective*

**although** *conjunction*

**amateur** *noun* amateurs

**ambition** *noun* ambitions

**ambulance** *noun* ambulances

**ambulanceman** *noun* ambulancemen

**American** *noun* Americans

**amount** *noun* amounts

**amount** *verb* amounts, amounting, amounted

**ancient\*** *adjective*

**angel** *noun* angels

> Spelling tip: an ELegant angEL

**angry** *adjective* angrier, angriest

**animal** *noun* animals

**animation\*** *noun* animations

**ankle** *noun* ankles

**anniversary\*** *noun* anniversaries

**announce\*** *verb* announces, announcing, announced

**announcement\*** *noun* announcements

**annoy** *verb* annoys, annoying, annoyed

**annual\*** *noun* annuals

**answer** *noun* answers

**answer** *verb* answers, answering, answered

**answerphone** *noun* answerphones

**ant** *noun* ants

**antique** *noun* antiques

**anybody** *pronoun*

**apartment** *noun* apartments

**apologize** *verb* apologizes, apologizing, apologized

This can also be spelt with *ise*

**apology\*** *noun* apologies

**apparent\*** *adjective*

**appear** *verb* appears, appearing, appeared

**appearance** *noun* appearances

**apple** *noun* apples

**application** *noun* applications

**apply** *verb* applies, applying, applied

**appointment\*** *noun* appointments

**appreciate** *verb* appreciates, appreciating, appreciated

**approach** *noun* approaches

**approach** *verb* approaches, approaching, approached

**approve** *verb* approves, approving, approved

**April** *noun*

**architect\*** *noun* architects

**architecture\*** *noun*

**are** *verb*

Do not confuse *are* and *our*, which some people pronounce in the same way

**area** *noun* areas

**aren't**

This is short for *are not*. Put the apostrophe between the *n* and the *t*

**argue** *verb* argues, arguing, argued

**argument** *noun* arguments

**arise** *verb* arising, arose, arisen

Do not confuse *arise* and *rise*. When an opportunity, problem or situation *arises*, it begins to exist: *A difficulty has arisen*. When someone or something *rises*, they move upward: *He rose to greet her*

**arm** *noun* arms

**arm** *verb* arms, arming, armed

**armchair** *noun* armchairs

**army** *noun* armies

**arrange** *verb* arranges, arranging, arranged

**arrangement** *noun* arrangements

**arrest** *noun* arrests

**arrest** *verb* arrests, arresting, arrested

**arrival** *noun* arrivals

**arrive** *verb* arrives, arriving, arrived

**art** *noun* arts

**article** *noun* articles

**artist** *noun* artists

**Asian** *noun* Asians

**ask** *verb* asks, asking, asked

**assistant** *noun* assistants

**at** *preposition*

**athlete** *noun* athletes

**atmosphere\*** *noun* atmospheres

**attach** *verb* attaches, attaching, attached

**attack** *noun* attacks

**attack** *verb* attacks, attacking, attacked

**attempt** *noun* attempts

**attempt** *verb* attempts, attempting, attempted

**attend** *verb* attends, attending, attended

**attention** *noun*

**attitude** *noun* attitudes

**attract** *verb* attracts, attracting, attracted

**attraction** *noun* attractions

**audience\*** *noun* audiences

**August** *noun*

**aunt** *noun* aunts

**author** *noun* authors

**author** *verb* authors, authoring, authored

**autumn** *noun* autumns

**available** *adjective*

**average** *noun* averages

**average** *verb* averages, averaging, averaged

**avoid** *verb* avoids, avoiding, avoided

**awake** *verb* awakes, awaking, awoke, awoken

**away** *adverb*

**awkward** *adjective*

# Bb

**baby** *noun* babies

**back** *noun* backs

**back** *verb* backs, backing, backed

**backache** *noun* backaches

**background** *noun* backgrounds

**backpack** *noun* backpacks

**backpacker** *noun* backpackers

**bacon** *noun*

**bad** *adjective* worse, worst

**badly** *adverb* worse, worst

**badminton\*** *noun*

**bag** *noun* bags

**bag** *verb* bags, bagging, bagged

**baggage** *noun*

**bake** *verb* bakes, baking, baked

**baker** *noun* bakers

**baking** *noun*

**balcony** *noun* balconies

**bald** *adjective* balder, baldest

**ball** *noun* balls

**ballet\*** *noun*

**balloon** *noun* balloons

**balloon** *verb* balloons, ballooning, ballooned

**banana** *noun* bananas

**band** *noun* bands

**band** *verb* bands, banding, banded

**bandage** *noun* bandages

**bandage** *verb* bandages, bandaging, bandaged

**bank** *noun* banks

**bank** *verb* banks, banking, banked

**bar** *noun* bars

**bar** *verb* bars, barring, barred

**barber** *noun* barbers

**bare** *adjective* barer, barest

> Do not confuse the adjective *bare* (naked or not covered) with the noun *bear* (the animal)

**bargain** *noun* bargains

**barman** *noun* barmen

**base** *noun* bases

> Do not confuse *base* with *bass*. The *base* of something is its lowest edge or part: *the base of my spine*. A *bass* is a male

singer who can sing very low notes. *Bass* instruments play low notes: *Suzi plays bass guitar*

**baseball** *noun* baseballs

**basic** *noun* basics

**basin** *noun* basins

**basket** *noun* baskets

**basketball** *noun* basketballs

**bass** *adjective* bass

**bass** *noun* basses

**bat** *noun* bats

**bat** *verb* bats, batting, batted

**bath** *noun* baths

**bathe** *verb* bathes, bathing, bathed

**bathroom** *noun* bathrooms

**battery** *noun* batteries

**battle** *noun* battles

**battle** *verb* battles, battling, battled

**bay** *noun* bays

**bay** *verb* bays, baying, bayed

**be** *verb* am, is, are, being, was, were, been

**beach** *noun* beaches

> Do not confuse the spellings of *beach* and *beech*: *a day at the beach; a forest of oak, ash, and beech*

**bean** *noun* beans

**bear** *noun* bears

**bear** *verb* bears, bearing, bore, borne

**beard** *noun* beards

**beat** *noun* beats

**beat** *verb* beats, beating, beat, beaten

**beautiful** *adjective*

**beauty** *noun* beauties

Spelling tip:
*Beautiful Elephants Are Usually Tiny*

**because** *conjunction*

Spelling tip:
*Betty Eats Cakes And Uses Seven Eggs*

**become** *verb* becomes, becoming, became, become

**bed** *noun* beds

**bedroom** *noun* bedrooms

**bee** *noun* bees

**beech** *noun* beeches

**beef** *noun*

**beer** *noun* beers

**begin** *verb* begins, beginning, began, begun

**beginner*** *noun* beginners

**beginning** *noun* beginnings

Remember that *beginning* has one g and two *n*s

**behave** *verb* behaves, behaving, behaved

**behaviour*** *noun*

**behind** *preposition*

**being** *noun* beings

**believe** *verb* believes, believing, believed

**bell** *noun* bells

**belong** *verb* belongs, belonging, belonged

**belt** *noun* belts

**belt** *verb* belts, belting, belted

**benefit** *noun* benefits

**benefit** *verb* benefits, benefiting, benefited

*Benefit* is spelt with two es, not two *is*

**berth** *noun* berths

Do not confuse the spellings of *berth* and *birth*: *The yacht has six berths; the birth of their daughter*

**beside** *preposition*

Do not confuse *beside* and *besides. Beside* means 'next to': *Put the spoon beside the knife. Besides* means 'in addition to' or 'as well': *He designs houses, offices and much else besides*

**besides** *preposition, adverb*

**best** *noun*

**better** *adjective, adverb*

**bicycle** *noun* bicycles

**bicycle** *verb* bicycles, bicycling, bicycled

**big** *adjective* bigger, biggest

**bike** *noun* bikes

**bike** *verb* bikes, biking, biked

**bill** *noun* bills

**bin** *noun* bins

**biography*** *noun* biographies

**biology*** *noun*

**bird** *noun* birds

**birth** *noun* births

**birthday** *noun* birthdays

**biscuit** *noun* biscuits

**bit** *noun* bits

**bite** *noun* bites

**bite** *verb* bites, biting, bit, bitten

**bitter** *adjective* bitterer, bitterest

**black** *adjective* blacker, blackest

When you are writing about a person or people, *Black* should start with a capital letter

**blackboard** *noun* blackboards

**blade** *noun* blades

**blame** *verb* blames, blaming, blamed

**blank** *adjective* blanker, blankest

**blank** *noun* blanks

**blanket** *noun* blankets

**bleed** *verb* bleeds, bleeding, bled

**blind** *adjective* blinder, blindest

**blind** *verb* blinds, blinding, blinded

**block** *noun* blocks

**block** *verb* blocks, blocking, blocked

**blog** *noun* blogs

**blog** *verb* blogs, blogging, blogged

**blogger** *noun* bloggers

**blonde** *adjective* blonder, blondest

**blonde** *noun* blondes

**blood** *noun*

**blouse** *noun* blouses

**blow** *noun* blows

**blow** *verb* blows, blowing, blew, blown

> Remember that the past tense of *blow* is *blew*. Don't confuse this with the colour *blue*

**blue** *adjective* bluer, bluest

**blue** *noun* blues

**board** *noun* boards

**board** *verb* boards, boarding, boarded

> Do not confuse the spellings of *board* and *bored*: The coin slipped between the boards in the kitchen floor; Lucy was bored without anyone to play with

**boat** *noun* boats

**body** *noun* bodies

**boil** *noun* boils

**boil** *verb* boils, boiling, boiled

**bold** *adjective* bolder, boldest

**bomb** *noun* bombs

**bomb** *verb* bombs, bombing, bombed

**bombing** *noun* bombings

**bone** *noun* bones

**bonnet** *noun* bonnets

**book** *noun* books

**book** *verb* books, booking, booked

**bookcase** *noun* bookcases

**bookseller** *noun* booksellers

**bookshelf** *noun* bookshelves

**bookshop** *noun* bookshops

**boot** *noun* boots

**border** *noun* borders

**border** *verb* borders, bordering, bordered

**bored** *adjective*

**boring** *adjective*

**borrow** *verb* borrows, borrowing, borrowed

**borrower** *noun* borrowers

**boss** *noun* bosses

**boss** *verb* bosses, bossing, bossed

**bother** *noun*

**bother** *verb* bothers, bothering, bothered

**bottle** *noun* bottles

**bottle** *verb* bottles, bottling, bottled

**bottom** *noun* bottoms

**bough\*** *noun* boughs

> Do not confuse *bough* and *bow*. A *bough* is a part of a tree and rhymes with 'wow'. A *bow* is a knot with loops and rhymes with 'no'. A *bow* is also the front of a ship and rhymes with 'cow'

**bought** *verb*

> Do not confuse *bought* and *brought*. *Bought* comes from *buy* and *brought* comes from *bring*

**bow** *noun* bows

**bow** *verb* bows, bowing, bowed

**bowl** *noun* bowls

**bowl** *verb* bowls, bowling, bowled

**box** *noun* boxes

**box** *verb* boxes, boxing, boxed

**boy** *noun* boys

**boyfriend** *noun* boyfriends

**bracelet** *noun* bracelets

**brain** *noun* brains

**brake** *noun* brakes

**brake** *verb* brakes, braking, braked

Do not confuse the spellings of *brake* and *break*, or *braking* and *breaking*

Spelling tip: *there's a rAKE in the brAKEs*

**branch** *noun* branches

**branch** *verb* branches, branching, branched

**brave** *adjective* braver, bravest

**brave** *noun* braves

**brave** *verb* braves, braving, braved

**bread** *noun*

**break** *noun* breaks

**break** *verb* breaks, breaking, broke, broken

Spelling tip: *you'll brEAK that Electrical Aerial, Kitty*

**breakfast** *noun* breakfasts

**breast** *noun* breasts

**breath** *noun* breaths

Do not confuse the spellings of the noun *breath* and the verb *breathe*: *I took a breath and then started to explain; Breathe deeply and count to ten*

**breathe** *verb* breathes, breathing, breathed

**breeze** *noun* breezes

**bride** *noun* brides

**bridge** *noun* bridges

**bridge** *verb* bridges, bridging, bridged

**brief** *adjective* briefer, briefest

**brief** *verb* briefs, briefing, briefed

**bright** *adjective* brighter, brightest

**bring** *verb* brings, bringing, brought

**broad** *adjective* broader, broadest

**brochure** *noun* brochures

**brother** *noun* brothers

**brought** *verb*

**brown** *noun* browns

**bruise** *noun* bruises

**bruise** *verb* bruises, bruising, bruised

**brush** *noun* brushes

**brush** *verb* brushes, brushing, brushed

**bucket** *noun* buckets

**bug** *noun* bugs

**bug** *verb* bugs, bugging, bugged

**build** *noun* builds

**build** *verb* builds, building, built

**builder** *noun* builders

**building** *noun* buildings

**bull** *noun* bulls

**bump** *noun* bumps

**bump** *verb* bumps, bumping, bumped

**bunch** *noun* bunches

**bunch** *verb* bunches, bunching, bunched

**burger** *noun* burgers

**burn** *noun* burns

**burn** *verb* burns, burning, burnt or burned

You can write either *burned* or *burnt* as the past form of *burn*

**burst** *noun* bursts

**burst** *verb* bursts, bursting, burst

**bury** *verb* buries, burying, buried

**bus** *noun* buses

**business*** *noun* businesses

**businessman*** *noun* businessmen

**businesswoman*** *noun* businesswomen

**busy** *adjective* busier, busiest

**busy** *verb* busies, busying, busied

**but** *noun* buts

**butcher** *noun* butchers

**butter** *noun* butters

**butter** *verb* butters, buttering, buttered

**butterfly** *noun* butterflies

**button** *noun* buttons

**button** *verb* buttons, buttoning, buttoned

**buy** *noun* buys

**buy** *verb* buys, buying, bought

**buyer** *noun* buyers

**by** *preposition*

Do not confuse *by* with *bye*: *A play by Shakespeare; Bye for now!*

**bye** *interjection*

# Cc

**cab** *noun* cabs

**cabbage** *noun* cabbages

**cafe** *noun* cafes

**cafeteria\*** *noun* cafeterias

**cage** *noun* cages

**cage** *verb* cages, caging, caged

**cake** *noun* cakes

**cake** *verb* cakes, caking, caked

**calculate** *verb* calculates, calculating, calculated

**calculator\*** *noun* calculators

**calendar** *noun* calendars

**calf** *noun* calves

**call** *noun* calls

**call** *verb* calls, calling, called

**calm** *adjective* calmer, calmest

**calm** *noun*

**calm** *verb* calms, calming, calmed

**calorie\*** *noun* calories

**camel** *noun* camels

**camera** *noun* cameras

**camp** *noun* camps

**camp** *verb* camps, camping, camped

**camping** *noun*

**can** *noun* cans

**can** *verb* cans, canning, canned

**canal** *noun* canals

**cancel** *verb* cancels, cancelling, cancelled

**cancer** *noun* cancers

**candidate** *noun* candidates

**candle** *noun* candles

**candy** *noun* candies

**canoe** *noun* canoes

**canoe** *verb* canoes, canoeing, canoed

**can't**

This is short for *can not*. Put the apostrophe between the *n* and the *t*.

**canteen** *noun* canteens

**cap** *noun* caps

**cap** *verb* caps, capping, capped

**capital** *noun* capitals

**captain** *noun* captains

**captain** *verb* captains, captaining, captained

**car** *noun* cars

**card** *noun* cards

**care** *noun* cares

**care** *verb* cares, caring, cared

**career** *noun* careers

**career** *verb* careers, careering, careered

**carpet** *noun* carpets

**carrot** *noun* carrots

**carry** *verb* carries, carrying, carried

**cartoon** *noun* cartoons

**case** *noun* cases

**cash** *noun* cash

**cashpoint** *noun* cashpoints

**casino** *noun* casinos

**castle** *noun* castles

**casual** *adjective*

**cat** *noun* cats

**catch** *noun* catches

**catch** *verb* catches, catching, caught

**category*** *noun* categories

**cave** *noun* caves

**CD-ROM** *noun* CD-ROMs

**ceiling** *noun* ceilings

**celebrate*** *verb* celebrates, celebrating, celebrated

**celebration*** *noun* celebrations

**celebrity*** *noun* celebrities

**cemetery*** *noun* cemeteries

**cent** *noun* cents

**centimetre*** *noun* centimetres

**centre** *noun* centres

**centre** *verb* centres, centring, centred

**century** *noun* centuries

**cereal** *noun* cereals

> Do not confuse the spellings of *cereal* and *serial*: *my favourite breakfast cereal; a new drama serial*

**ceremony** *noun* ceremonies

**certain** *adjective*

**certificate*** *noun* certificates

**chain** *noun* chains

**chain** *verb* chains, chaining, chained

**chair** *noun* chairs

**chair** *verb* chairs, chairing, chaired

**challenge** *noun* challenges

**challenge** *verb* challenges, challenging, challenged

**champagne*** *noun* champagnes

**champion** *noun* champions

**champion** *verb* champions, championing, championed

**championship** *noun* championships

**chance** *noun* chances

**chance** *verb* chances, chancing, chanced

**change** *noun* changes

**change** *verb* changes, changing, changed

**channel** *noun* channels

**channel** *verb* channels, channelling, channelled

**chapter** *noun* chapters

**character*** *noun* characters

**charge** *noun* charges

**charge** *verb* charges, charging, charged

**charity** *noun* charities

**chat** *noun* chats

**chat** *verb* chats, chatting, chatted

**cheap** *adjective* cheaper, cheapest

**check** *noun* checks

**check** *verb* checks, checking, checked

**check-in** *noun* check-ins

**check-out** *noun* check-outs

**cheek** *noun* cheeks

**cheer** *noun* cheers

**cheer** *verb* cheers, cheering, cheered

**cheese** *noun* cheeses

**chef** *noun* chefs

**chemist** *noun* chemists

**chemistry*** *noun*

**cheque** *noun* cheques

**chess** *noun*

**chicken** *noun* chickens

**child** *noun* children

**childhood** *noun* childhoods

**chilli** *noun* chillies

**chimney** *noun* chimneys

**chin** *noun* chins

**Chinese** *adjective*

**chip** *noun* chips

**chip** *verb* chips, chipping, chipped

**chocolate** *noun* chocolates

**choice** *adjective* choicer, choicest

**choice** *noun* choices

**choose** *verb* chooses, choosing, chose, chosen

**chord** *noun* chords

Do not confuse the spellings of *chord* and *cord*. A *chord* is a number of musical notes played at the same time and a *cord* is a thin rope

**Christmas** *noun* Christmases

**church** *noun* churches

**cigar** *noun* cigars

**cigarette** *noun* cigarettes

**cinema** *noun* cinemas

**circle** *noun* circles

**circle** *verb* circles, circling, circled

**circus** *noun* circuses

**city** *noun* cities

**clap** *noun* claps

**clap** *verb* claps, clapping, clapped

**class** *noun* classes

**class** *verb* classes, classing, classed

**classmate** *noun* classmates

**classroom** *noun* classrooms

**clean** *adjective* cleaner, cleanest

**clean** *verb* cleans, cleaning, cleaned

**cleaner** *noun* cleaners

**clear** *adjective* clearer, clearest

**clear** *verb* clears, clearing, cleared

**clever** *adjective* cleverer, cleverest

**click** *noun* clicks

**click** *verb* clicks, clicking, clicked

**climate** *noun* climates

**climb** *noun* climbs

**climb** *verb* climbs, climbing, climbed

**clock** *noun* clocks

**close** *adjective* closer, closest

**close** *verb* closes, closing, closed

The adjective *close* is said with an s sound. The verb *close* is said with a z sound, like 'rose'.

**cloud** *noun* clouds

**cloud** *verb* clouds, clouding, clouded

**cloudy** *adjective* cloudier, cloudiest

**clown** *noun* clowns

**clown** *verb* clowns, clowning, clowned

**club** *noun* clubs

**club** *verb* clubs, clubbing, clubbed

**coach** *noun* coaches

**coach** *verb* coaches, coaching, coached

**coarse** *adjective* coarser, coarsest

Do not confuse *coarse* with *course*. *Coarse* is an adjective: *The sand was very coarse; His manners are coarse.* *Course* is a noun: *The plane changed course: a course in art history*

**coast** *noun* coasts

**coast** *verb* coasts, coasting, coasted

**coat** *noun* coats

**coat** *verb* coats, coating, coated

**coconut** *noun* coconuts

**coffee** *noun* coffees

**coin** *noun* coins

**coin** *verb* coins, coining, coined

**cold** *adjective* colder, coldest

**collar** *noun* collars

**colleague*** *noun* colleagues

**collect** *verb* collects, collecting, collected

**collecting** *noun*

**collection** *noun* collections

**college** *noun* colleges

**colour** *noun* colours

**colour** *verb* colours, colouring, coloured

**colouring** *noun*

**comb** *noun* combs

**comb** *verb* combs, combing, combed

**come** *verb* comes, coming, came, come

Remember that the past tense of *come* is *came* and the past participle is *come*

**comedy** *noun* comedies

**comic** *noun* comics

**comma** *noun* commas

**comment** *noun* comments

**comment** *verb* comments, commenting, commented

**committee*** *noun* committees

**common** *adjective* commoner, commonest

**common** *noun* commons

**communicate** *verb* communicates, communicating, communicated

**communication** *noun* communications

**community** *noun* communities

**company** *noun* companies

**comparative** *noun* comparatives

**compare** *verb* compares, comparing, compared

**compete** *verb* competes, competing, competed

**competition*** *noun* competitions

**competitor** *noun* competitors

**complain** *verb* complains, complaining, complained

**complaint** *noun* complaints

**complete** *verb* completes, completing, completed

**complement** *noun* complements

**complement** *verb* complements, complementing, complemented

Do not confuse *complement* with *compliment*: *The wine complemented the food; She complimented me on my work*

**compliment** *noun* compliments

**compliment** *verb* compliments, complimenting, complimented

**composition** *noun* compositions

**computer** *noun* computers

**concentrate*** *noun* concentrates

**concentrate*** *verb* concentrates, concentrating, concentrated

**concert** *noun* concerts

**concert** *verb* concerts, concerting, concerted

**conclusion*** *noun* conclusions

**condition** *noun* conditions

**conference*** *noun* conferences

**confident** *adjective*

**confirm** *verb* confirms, confirming, confirmed

**connect** *verb* connects, connecting, connected

**conscience*** *noun*

**conscious*** *adjective*

**consider** *verb* considers, considering, considered

**consist** *verb* consists, consisting, consisted

**consonant*** *noun* consonants

**contact** *noun* contacts

**contact** *verb* contacts, contacting, contacted

**contain** *verb* contains, containing, contained

**content** *noun* contents

**content** *verb* contents, contenting, contented

**contest** *noun* contests

**contest** *verb* contests, contesting, contested

**continent*** *noun* continents

**continual** *adjective*

Do not confuse *continual* with *continuous*. *Continual* means that something happens repeatedly and without interruption: *I'm fed up with this continual noise*. *Continuous* is only used for things that happen without interruption and do not stop at all: *He has a continuous buzzing sound in his ear*

**continue** *verb* continues, continuing, continued

**continuous\*** *adjective*

**contract** *noun* contracts

**contract** *verb* contracts, contracting, contracted

**control** *noun* controls

**control** *verb* controls, controlling, controlled

**controversy** *noun* controversies

**convenience** *noun* conveniences

**conversation\*** *noun* conversations

**convince** *verb* convinces, convincing, convinced

**cook** *noun* cooks

**cook** *verb* cooks, cooking, cooked

**cooker** *noun* cookers

**cool** *adjective* cooler, coolest

**cool** *verb* cools, cooling, cooled

**copy** *noun* copies

**copy** *verb* copies, copying, copied

**cord** *noun* cords

Do not confuse the spellings of *cord* and *chord*. A *cord* is a thin rope and a *chord* is a number of musical notes played at the same time

**corn** *noun* corns

**corner** *noun* corners

**corner** *verb* corners, cornering, cornered

**correct** *verb* corrects, correcting, corrected

**correction** *noun* corrections

**correspond** *verb* corresponds, corresponding, corresponded

**corridor\*** *noun* corridors

**cost** *noun* costs

**cost** *verb* costs, costing, cost, costed

**cosy** *adjective* cosier, cosiest

**cosy** *noun* cosies

**cottage** *noun* cottages

**cotton** *noun* cottons

**cough\*** *noun* coughs

**cough\*** *verb* coughs, coughing, coughed

**could** *verb*

**couldn't**

This is short for *could not*. Put the apostrophe between the *n* and the *t*

**councillor** *noun* councillors

Do not confuse *councillor* with *counsellor*. A *councillor* is an official in a local council. A *counsellor* gives people advice on personal matters

**counsellor** *noun* counsellors

**count** *noun* counts

**count** *verb* counts, counting, counted

**country** *noun* countries

**couple** *noun* couples

**couple** *verb* couples, coupling, coupled

**course** *noun* courses

Do not confuse *course* with *coarse*. *Course* is a noun: *The plane changed course; a course in art history*. *Coarse* is an adjective meaning: *The sand was very coarse; His manners are coarse*

**court** *noun* courts

**court** *verb* courts, courting, courted

**cousin** *noun* cousins

**cover** *noun* covers

**cover** *verb* covers, covering, covered

**cow** *noun* cows

**cracker** *noun* crackers

**crash** *noun* crashes

**crash** *verb* crashes, crashing, crashed

**crazy** *adjective* crazier, craziest

**cream** *noun* creams

**create** *verb* creates, creating, created

**creature** *noun* creatures

**credit** *noun* credits

**credit** *verb* credit, crediting, credited

**crew** *noun* crews

**crew** *verb* crews, crewing, crewed

**cricket** *noun* crickets

**crime** *noun* crimes

**criminal** *noun* criminals

**crisp** *adjective* crisper, crispest

**crisp** *noun* crisps

**criticize** *verb* criticizes, criticizing, criticized

This can also be spelt with *-ise*

**crop** *noun* crops

**crop** *verb* crops, cropping, cropped

**cross** *noun* crosses

**cross** *verb* crosses, crossing, crossed

**crossing** *noun* crossings

**crowd** *noun* crowds

**crowd** *verb* crowds, crowding, crowded

**cruel** *adjective* crueller, cruellest

**cruise** *noun* cruises

**cruise** *verb* cruises, cruising, cruised

**cry** *noun* cries

**cry** *verb* cries, crying, cried

**cucumber** *noun* cucumbers

**culture** *noun* cultures

**cue** *noun* cues

Do not confuse the spellings of *cue* and *queue*: That's the lead singer's cue; a long queue at the bank

**cup** *noun* cups

**cup** *verb* cups, cupping, cupped

**cupboard** *noun* cupboards

**curiosity*** *noun* curiosities

**curly** *adjective* curlier, curliest

**currant** *noun* currants

Do not confuse *currant* with *current*. A *currant* is a dried grape. Something that is *current* is happening now. A *current* is also a flow of air, water or electricity

**current** *noun* currents

**curriculum*** *noun* curricula or curriculums

**curry** *noun* curries

**cursor** *noun* cursors

**curtain** *noun* curtains

**cushion** *noun* cushions

**cushion** *verb* cushions, cushioning, cushioned

**custom** *noun* customs

**customer** *noun* customers

**cut** *noun* cuts

**cut** *verb* cuts, cutting, cut

**cycle** *noun* cycles

**cycle** *verb* cycles, cycling, cycled

**cyclist** *noun* cyclists

# Dd

**dad** *noun* dads

**daddy** *noun* daddies

**daily** *adjective*

**dairy** *noun* dairies

**damage** *noun* damages

**damage** *verb* damages, damaging, damaged

**damn** *verb* damns, damning, damned

**dance** *noun* dances

**dance** *verb* dances, dancing, danced

**dancer** *noun* dancers

**danger** *noun* dangers

**dark** *adjective* darker, darkest

**date** *noun* dates

**date** *verb* dates, dating, dated

**daughter** *noun* daughters

**day** *noun* days

**deaf** *adjective* deafer, deafest

**dear** *adjective* dearer, dearest

**dear** *noun* dears

Do not confuse *dear* with *deer*. *Dear* means expensive or loved. A *deer* is an animal

**death** *noun* deaths

**debt** *noun* debts

**December** *noun*

**decide** *verb* decides, deciding, decided

**decision\*** *noun* decisions

**decorate\*** *verb* decorates, decorating, decorated

**decrease** *noun* decreases

**decrease** *verb* decreases, decreasing, decreased

**deep** *adjective* deeper, deepest

**defeat** *noun* defeats

**defeat** *verb* defeats, defeating, defeated

**defence** *noun* defences

**defend** *verb* defends, defending, defended

**definite** *adjective*

There is no *a* in *definite* or *definitely*. Spelling tip: *inFINITy is deFINITe*

Do not confuse *definite* and *definitive*. If something is *definite*, it is firm and clear and not likely to be changed: *Do we have a definite date for the meeting?* Something that is *definitive* is accepted by everyone as being correct: *No one has come up with a definitive answer*

**definitive** *adjective*

**degree** *noun* degrees

**delay** *noun* delays

**delay** *verb* delays, delaying, delayed

**delete** *verb* deletes, deleting, deleted

**deliberate\*** *verb* deliberates, deliberating, deliberated

**deliver** *verb* delivers, delivering, delivered

**delivery\*** *noun* deliveries

**demand** *noun* demands

**demand** *verb* demands, demanding, demanded

**dentist** *noun* dentists

**depart** *verb* departs, departing, departed

**department** *noun* departments

**departure** *noun* departures

**depend** *verb* depends, depending, depended

**dependant** *noun* dependants

Do not confuse *dependant* and *dependent*. Your *dependants* are the people you are financially responsible for: *He is unmarried and has no dependants*. If you are *dependent* on someone or something, you rely on them: *Their economy is dependent on oil*

**dependent** *adjective*

**depth** *noun* depths

**describe** *verb* describes, describing, described

**description\*** *noun* descriptions

**desert** *noun* deserts

**desert** *verb* deserts, deserting, deserted

Do not confuse the spellings of *desert* and *dessert*: *The residents are ready to desert the city; What would you like for dessert?*

**deserve** *verb* deserves, deserving, deserved

**design** *noun* designs

**design** *verb* designs, designing, designed

**designer** *noun* designers

**desk** *noun* desks

**desperate** *adjective*

**despite** *preposition*

**dessert** *noun* desserts

**destination*** *noun* destinations

**destroy** *verb* destroys, destroying, destroyed

**detail** *noun* details

**detective** *noun* detectives

**determined** *adjective*

**develop** *verb* develops, developing, developed

**development*** *noun* developments

**device** *noun* devices

Do not confuse the spellings of the noun *device* and the verb *devise*: *a device for picking up litter; They need to devise a new plan to deal with unemployment*

**diagram** *noun* diagrams

**dial** *noun* dials

**dial** *verb* dials, dialling, dialled

**diary** *noun* diaries

Do not confuse the order of the vowels in *diary* and *dairy*

**dictionary** *noun* dictionaries

**didn't**

This is short for *did not*. Put the apostrophe between the *n* and the *t*

**die** *verb* dies, dying, died

Change the *ie* to *y* and add *ing* for *dying*

**diet** *noun* diets

**diet** *verb* diets, dieting, dieted

**difference** *noun* differences

**different** *adjective*

**difficult** *adjective*

**difficulty*** *noun* difficulties

**dig** *noun* digs

**dig** *verb* digs, digging, dug

**digital** *adjective*

**dinner** *noun* dinners

**dinosaur*** *noun* dinosaurs

**diploma** *noun* diplomas

**direct** *verb* directs, directing, directed

**direction** *noun* directions

**director** *noun* directors

**dirty** *adjective* dirtier, dirtiest

**dirty** *verb* dirties, dirtying, dirtied

**disadvantage*** *noun* disadvantages

**disagree** *verb* disagrees, disagreeing, disagreed

**disappear** *verb* disappears, disappearing, disappeared

**disappoint*** *verb* disappoints, disappointing, disappointed

**disappointment*** *noun* disappointments

**disaster** *noun* disasters

**disastrous** *adjective*

**disc** *noun* discs

**discipline** *noun* disciplines

**discipline** *verb* disciplines, disciplining, disciplined

**disco** *noun* discos

**discount** *noun* discounts

**discount** *verb* discounts, discounting, discounted

**discover** *verb* discovers, discovering, discovered

**discreet*** *adjective*

Do not confuse *discreet* and *discrete*. If you are *discreet*, you are careful to avoid attracting attention or revealing private information: *I made a few discreet inquiries about her*. If things are *discrete*, they are not joined or connected in any way: *I met him on three discrete occasions*

**discrete*** *adjective*

**discuss*** *verb* discusses, discussing, discussed

**discussion\*** *noun* discussions

**disease** *noun* diseases

**dish** *noun* dishes

**dish** *verb* dishes, dishing, dished

**dishcloth** *noun* dishcloths

**dishwasher** *noun* dishwashers

**disk** *noun* disks

**dislike** *noun* dislikes

**dislike** *verb* dislikes, disliking, disliked

**display** *noun* displays

**display** *verb* displays, displaying, displayed

**distance** *noun* distances

**distance** *verb* distances, distancing, distanced

**district** *noun* districts

**disturb** *verb* disturbs, disturbing, disturbed

**dive** *noun* dives

**dive** *verb* dives, diving, dived

**diver** *noun* divers

**divide** *verb* divides, dividing, divided

**diving** *noun*

**divorce** *noun* divorces

**divorce** *verb* divorces, divorcing, divorced

**DJ** *noun* DJs

**do** *verb* does, doing, did, done

**doctor** *noun* doctors

**doctor** *verb* doctors, doctoring, doctored

**document** *noun* documents

**document** *verb* documents, documenting, documented

**documentary\*** *noun* documentaries

**doesn't**

This is short for *does not*. Put the apostrophe between the *n* and the *t*

**dog** *noun* dogs

**dog** *verb* dogs, dogging, dogged

**doll** *noun* dolls

**dollar** *noun* dollars

**donkey** *noun* donkeys

**don't**

This is short for *do not*. Put the apostrophe between the *n* and the *t*

**door** *noun* doors

**dot** *noun* dots

**dot** *verb* dots, dotting, dotted

**double** *noun* doubles

**double** *verb* doubles, doubling, doubled

**double-click** *verb* double-clicks, double-clicking, double-clicked

**doubt\*** *noun* doubts

**doubt\*** *verb* doubts, doubting, doubted

**down** *verb* downs, downing, downed

**download** *verb* downloads, downloading, downloaded

**dozen** *noun* dozens

**draft** *noun* drafts

**draft** *verb* drafts, drafting, drafted

Do not confuse *draft* with *draught*. A *draft* is a first version of a speech or book, and to *draft* something is to complete a version of it. A *draught* is a current of air

**drag** *verb* drags, dragging, dragged

**drama** *noun* dramas

**draught** *noun* draughts

**draw** *verb* draws, drawing, drew, drawn

**drawer** *noun* drawers

**drawing** *noun* drawings

**dream** *noun* dreams

**dream** *verb* dreams, dreaming, dreamt or dreamed

**dress** *noun* dresses

**dress** *verb* dresses, dressing, dressed

**drink** *noun* drinks

**drink** *verb* drinks, drinking, drank, drunk

**drive** *noun* drives

**drive** *verb* drives, driving, drove, driven

**driver** *noun* drivers

**drop** *noun* drops

**drop** *verb* drops, dropping, dropped

**drove** *noun* droves

**drum** *noun* drums

**drum** *verb* drums, drumming, drummed

**drunk** *adjective* drunker, drunkest

**drunk** *noun* drunks

**dry** *adjective* drier or dryer, driest or dryest

**dry** *verb* dries, drying, dried

**duck** *noun* ducks

**duck** *verb* ducks, ducking, ducked

**due** *adjective*

**dug** *verb*

**dull** *adjective* duller, dullest

**dull** *verb* dulls, dulling, dulled

**dust** *verb* dusts, dusting, dusted

**dustbin** *noun* dustbins

**dusty** *adjective* dustier, dustiest

**duty** *noun* duties

**duvet** *noun* duvets

**DVD** *noun* DVDs

# Ee

**ear** *noun* ears

**early** *adjective* earlier, earliest

**earn** *verb* earns, earning, earned

**earring** *noun* earrings

**earth** *noun*

**east** *noun*

**easy** *adjective* easier, easiest

**eat** *verb* eats, eating, ate, eaten

 Remember that the past tense of *eat* is *ate*

**edge** *noun* edges

**edge** *verb* edges, edging, edged

**education** *noun* educations

**effect** *noun* effects

Do not confuse the spelling of the noun *effect* with the verb *affect*. Something that *affects* you has an *effect* on you

**effort** *noun* efforts

**egg** *noun* eggs

**eight** *noun* eights

**eighteen** *noun* eighteens

**eighteenth** *noun* eighteenths

**eighth** *noun* eighths

**eightieth** *noun* eightieths

**eighty** *noun* eighties

**elbow** *noun* elbows

**elbow** *verb* elbows, elbowing, elbowed

**elder** *noun* elders

**elder** *adjective*

Do not confuse *elder* and *older*. *Elder* is used when you are saying which of two people was born first. It is not used with *than*: *I live with my elder sister*; *He is the elder of the two*. *Older* simply means 'more old', and can be used of people or things, and can be followed by *than*: *My car is older than yours*

**election** *noun* elections

**electric** *noun* electrics

**element** *noun* elements

**elephant\*** *noun* elephants

**elevator** *noun* elevators

**eleven** *noun* elevens

**eleventh** *noun* elevenths

**e-mail** *noun* e-mails

**e-mail** *verb* e-mails, e-mailing, e-mailed

**embarrass\*** *verb* embarrasses, embarrassing, embarrassed

**embassy\*** *noun* embassies

**emergency\*** *noun* emergencies

**emphasis** *noun* emphases

**employ** *verb* employs, employing, employed

**employee** *noun* employees

**employer** *noun* employers

**employment** *noun*

**empty** *adjective* emptier, emptiest

**empty** *verb* empties, emptying, emptied

**encourage** *verb* encourages, encouraging, encouraged

**end** *noun* ends

**end** *verb* ends, ending, ended

**ending** *noun* endings

**enemy** *noun* enemies

**energy** *noun* energies

**engine** *noun* engines

**engineer** *noun* engineers

**engineer** *verb* engineers, engineering, engineered

**enjoy** *verb* enjoys, enjoying, enjoyed

**enough** *adverb*

**enter** *verb* enters, entering, entered

**entertain** *verb* entertains, entertaining, entertained

**entertainment\*** *noun* entertainments

**entrance** *noun* entrances

**entrance** *verb* entrances, entrancing, entranced

**entry** *noun* entries

**envelope** *noun* envelopes

**environment** *noun* environments

> There is an *n* before the *m* in *environment*

**equal** *noun* equals

**equal** *verb* equals, equalling, equalled

**equip** *verb* equips, equipping, equipped

**equipment** *noun*

**eraser** *noun* erasers

**escape** *noun* escapes

**escape** *verb* escapes, escaping, escaped

**especially** *adverb*

**essay** *noun* essays

**essential\*** *noun* essentials

**euro** *noun* euros

**European** *noun* Europeans

**even** *adjective*

**even** *verb* evens, evening, evened

**evening** *noun* evenings

**event** *noun* events

**exact** *verb* exacts, exacting, exacted

**exaggerate\*** *verb* exaggerates, exaggerating, exaggerated

**exam** *noun* exams

**examination** *noun* examinations

**examiner** *noun* examiners

**example** *noun* examples

**excellent** *adjective*

**except** *preposition*

> Do not confuse the spellings of *except* and *accept*: He works every day except Tuesday; Please accept my apologies

**exchange** *noun* exchanges

**exchange** *verb* exchanges, exchanging, exchanged

**excite** *verb* excites, exciting, excited

**excitement** *noun*

**excuse** *noun* excuses

**excuse** *verb* excuses, excusing, excused

**exercise** *noun* exercises

**exercise** *verb* exercises, exercising, exercised

**exhibition** *noun* exhibitions

**exist** *verb* exists, existing, existed

**existence\*** *noun* existences

**exit** *noun* exits

**exit** *verb* exits, exiting, exited

**expect** *verb* expects, expecting, expected

**expedition\*** *noun*
expeditions

**experience** *noun*
experiences

**experience** *verb*
experiences, experiencing,
experienced

**experiment\*** *noun*
experiments

**experiment\*** *verb*
experiments,
experimenting,
experimented

**expert** *noun* experts

**explain** *verb* explains,
explaining, explained

**explanation** *noun*
explanations

**explode** *verb* explodes,
exploding, exploded

**explore** *verb* explores,
exploring, explored

**explorer** *noun* explorers

**explosion** *noun* explosions

**extra** *noun* extras

**extreme** *noun* extremes

**eye** *noun* eyes

**eye** *verb* eyes, eyeing or
eying, eyed

# Ff

**face** *noun* faces

**face** *verb* faces, facing,
faced

**fact** *noun* facts

**factory** *noun* factories

**fail** *noun* fails

**fail** *verb* fails, failing, failed

**fair** *adjective* fairer, fairest

**fair** *noun* fairs

**fall** *noun* falls

**fall** *verb* falls, falling, fell,
fallen

> Remember that
> the past tense of
> *fall* is *fell*

**false** *adjective* falser,
falsest

**familiar** *adjective*

**family** *noun* families

**famous** *adjective*

**fan** *noun* fans

**fan** *verb* fans, fanning,
fanned

**fancy** *adjective* fancier,
fanciest

**fancy** *noun* fancies

**fancy** *verb* fancies,
fancying, fancied

**fantastic** *noun*

**far** *adjective* farther or
further, farthest or furthest

**fare** *noun* fares

**fare** *verb* fares, faring, fared

**farm** *noun* farms

**farm** *verb* farms, farming,
farmed

**farmer** *noun* farmers

**fashion** *noun* fashions

**fashion** *verb* fashions,
fashioning, fashioned

**fast** *adjective* faster, fastest

**fast** *noun* fasts

**fast** *verb* fasts, fasting,
fasted

**fasten** *verb* fastens,
fastening, fastened

**fat** *adjective* fatter, fattest

**fat** *noun* fats

**father** *noun* fathers

**father** *verb* fathers,
fathering, fathered

**fault** *noun* faults

**fault** *verb* faults, faulting,
faulted

**favour** *noun* favours

**favour** *verb* favours,
favouring, favoured

**favourite** *noun* favourites

**fax** *noun* faxes

**fax** *verb* faxes, faxing, faxed

**fear** *noun* fears

**fear** *verb* fears, fearing,
feared

**feat** *noun* feats

> Do not confuse *feat*
> with *feet*. A *feat* is an
> achievement. *Feet* is
> the plural of *foot*

**February** *noun*

**fed** *verb*

**fee** *noun* fees

**feed** *noun* feeds

**feed** *verb* feeds, feeding, fed

**feel** *verb* feels, feeling, felt

Remember that the past tense of *feel* is *felt*

**feeling** *noun* feelings

**feet** *plural noun*

**fell** *verb*

**felt** *noun*

**female** *noun* females

**ferry** *noun* ferries

**ferry** *verb* ferries, ferrying, ferried

**festival** *noun* festivals

**fetch** *verb* fetches, fetching, fetched

**fever** *noun* fevers

**few** *adjective* fewer, fewest

**fiction** *noun* fictions

**field** *noun* fields

**field** *verb* fields, fielding, fielded

**fifteen** *noun* fifteens

**fifteenth** *noun* fifteenths

**fifth** *noun* fifths

**fiftieth** *noun* fiftieths

**fifty** *noun* fifties

**fight** *noun* fights

**fight** *verb* fights, fighting, fought

Remember that the past tense of *fight* is *fought*

**figure** *noun* figures

**figure** *verb* figures, figuring, figured

**file** *noun* files

**file** *verb* files, filing, filed

**fill** *verb* fills, filling, filled

**film** *noun* films

**film** *verb* films, filming, filmed

**final** *noun* finals

Do not confuse the spellings of *final* and *finale*: Nathan will miss the cup final; All the dancers were on stage for the finale

**finale** *noun* finales

**find** *noun* finds

**find** *verb* finds, finding, found

**fine** *adjective* finer, finest

**fine** *noun* fines

**fine** *verb* fines, fining, fined

**finger** *noun* fingers

**finger** *verb* fingers, fingering, fingered

**finish** *noun* finishes

**finish** *verb* finishes, finishing, finished

**fire** *noun* fires

**fire** *verb* fires, firing, fired

**fireman** *noun* firemen

**firm** *adjective* firmer, firmest

**firm** *noun* firms

**first** *noun* firsts

**fish** *noun* fish or fishes

**fish** *verb* fishes, fishing, fished

**fisherman** *noun* fishermen

**fit** *adjective* fitter, fittest

**fit** *noun* fits

**fit** *verb* fits, fitting, fitted

**five** *noun* fives

**fix** *noun* fixes

**fix** *verb* fixes, fixing, fixed

**flag** *noun* flags

**flag** *verb* flags, flagging, flagged

**flame** *noun* flames

**flat** *adjective* flatter, flattest

**flat** *noun* flats

**flavour** *noun* flavours

**flavour** *verb* flavours, flavouring, flavoured

**flea** *noun* fleas

**flee** *verb* flees, fleeing, fled

Do not confuse the spellings of *flee* and *flea*. To *flee* is to run away. A *flea* is a small insect

**flew** *verb*

Do not confuse the spellings of *flew* and *flue*: I flew home last week; The flue needs cleaned

**flight** *noun* flights

**float** *noun* floats

**float** verb floats, floating, floated

**flood** noun floods

**flood** verb floods, flooding, flooded

**floor** noun floors

**floor** verb floors, flooring, floored

**flour** noun flours

> Do not confuse the spellings of *flour* and *flower: You need flour to make bread; The tulip is my favourite flower*

**flow** noun flows

**flow** verb flows, flowing, flowed

**flower** noun flowers

**flower** verb flowers, flowering, flowered

**flue** noun flues

**flute** noun flutes

**fly** noun flies

**fly** verb flies, flying, flew, flown

**fog** noun fogs

**fold** noun folds

**fold** verb folds, folding, folded

**folder** noun folders

**folk** noun folk or folks

**follow** verb follows, following, followed

**following** noun followings

**fond** adjective fonder, fondest

**food** noun foods

**fool** noun fools

**fool** verb fools, fooling, fooled

**foot** noun feet

**foot** verb foots, footing, footed

**football** noun footballs

**footballer** noun footballers

**force** noun forces

**force** verb forces, forcing, forced

**forecast** noun forecasts

**forecast** verb forecasts, forecasting, forecast or forecasted

**forehead** noun foreheads

**foreign\*** adjective

**foreigner\*** noun foreigners

**forest** noun forests

**forget** verb forgets, forgetting, forgot, forgotten

**forgive** verb forgives, forgiving, forgave, forgiven

**fork** noun forks

**fork** verb forks, forking, forked

**form** noun forms

**form** verb forms, forming, formed

**former** adjective

**forth** adverb

**fortieth** noun fortieths

**fortnight** noun fortnights

**forty** noun forties

**forward** verb forwards, forwarding, forwarded

**found** verb founds, founding, founded

**fountain** noun fountains

**four** noun fours

**fourteen** noun fourteens

**fourth** noun fourths

> Do not confuse the spellings of *fourth* and *forth: This is the fourth time you have been late; They set forth at the beginning of June*

**frame** noun frames

**frame** verb frames, framing, framed

**free** adjective freer, freest

**free** verb frees, freeing, freed

**freeze** verb freezes, freezing, froze, frozen

> Do not confuse the spellings of *freeze* and *frieze: Freeze raw meat on the day you buy it; an intricate plaster frieze*

**freezer** noun freezers

**frequent** verb frequents, frequenting, frequented

**frequently** adverb

**fresh** *adjective* fresher, freshest

**Friday** *noun* Fridays

> Spelling tip: *I always visit my FRIend on a FRIday*

**fridge** *noun* fridges

**friend** *noun* friends

**friendly** *adjective* friendlier, friendliest

**friendship** *noun* friendships

**frieze** *noun* friezes

**frog** *noun* frogs

**front** *noun* fronts

**fruit** *noun* fruits

**fry** *noun* fries

**fry** *verb* fries, frying, fried

**fuel** *noun* fuels

**fuel** *verb* fuels, fuelling, fuelled

**full** *adjective* fuller, fullest

**fun** *noun*

**funny** *adjective* funnier, funniest

**fur** *noun* furs

**further** *verb* furthers, furthering, furthered

**future** *noun* futures

# Gg

**gain** *noun* gains

**gain** *verb* gains, gaining, gained

**gallery** *noun* galleries

**game** *adjective* gamer, gamest

**game** *noun* games

**game** *verb* games, gaming, gamed

**gap** *noun* gaps

**garage** *noun* garages

**garden** *noun* gardens

**garden** *verb* gardens, gardening, gardened

**gas** *noun* gases

**gas** *verb* gasses, gassing, gassed

> The plural of the noun *gas* is *gases*. The verb forms of *gas* are spelt with a double *s*

**gate** *noun* gates

**gay** *adjective* gayer, gayest

**gay** *noun* gays

**general** *noun* generals

**generation*** *noun* generations

**gentle** *adjective* gentler, gentlest

**geography*** *noun*

**German** *noun* Germans

**get** *verb* gets, getting, got

**ghost** *noun* ghosts

**giant** *noun* giants

**gift** *noun* gifts

**gift** *verb* gifts, gifting, gifted

**giraffe*** *noun* giraffes

**girl** *noun* girls

**girlfriend** *noun* girlfriends

**give** *verb* gives, giving, gave, given

**glad** *adjective* gladder, gladdest

**glance** *noun* glances

**glance** *verb* glances, glancing, glanced

**glass** *noun* glasses

**glove** *noun* gloves

**go** *noun* goes

**go** *verb* goes, going, went, gone

> Remember that the past tense of *go* is *went*

**goal** *noun* goals

**goalkeeper** *noun* goalkeepers

**goat** *noun* goats

**god** *noun* gods

**gold** *noun*

**golf** *verb* golfs, golfing, golfed

**golfer** *noun* golfers

**good** *adjective* better, best

**good** *noun* goods

**goodbye** *interjection*

**government*** *noun* governments

**grab** *noun* grabs

**grab** *verb* grabs, grabbing, grabbed

**grade** *noun* grades

**grade** *verb* grades, grading, graded

**graduation\*** *noun* graduations

**gram** *noun* grams

**grammar\*** *noun*

**grandad** *noun* grandads

**grandchild** *noun* grandchildren

**granddaughter** *noun* granddaughters

**grandfather** *noun* grandfathers

**grandma** *noun* grandmas

**grandmother** *noun* grandmothers

**grandpa** *noun* grandpas

**grandparent** *noun* grandparents

**grandson** *noun* grandsons

**granny** *noun* grannies

**grant** *noun* grants

**grant** *verb* grants, granting, granted

**grape** *noun* grapes

**grapefruit** *noun* grapefruits or grapefruit

**grass** *noun* grasses

**grate** *noun* grates

**grate** *verb* grates, grating, grated

**great** *adjective* greater, greatest

Do not confuse the spellings of *great* and *grate*: *the great Amazon River; the fire behind the grate; Grate 250g of cheddar*

**Greek** *noun* Greeks

**green** *adjective* greener, greenest

**green** *noun* greens

**greengrocer** *noun* greengrocers

**greet** *verb* greets, greeting, greeted

**greeting** *noun* greetings

**grey** *adjective* greyer, greyest

**grey** *noun* greys

**grey** *verb* greys, greying, greyed

**grill** *noun* grills

**grill** *verb* grills, grilling, grilled

Do not confuse the spellings of *grill* and *grille*: *Brown the bread under the grill for a minute; a well covered with an iron grille*

**grille** *noun* grilles

**grocer** *noun* grocers

**grocery** *noun* groceries

**groom** *noun* grooms

**groom** *verb* grooms, grooming, groomed

**ground** *noun* grounds

**ground** *verb* grounds, grounding, grounded

**group** *noun* groups

**group** *verb* groups, grouping, grouped

**grow** *verb* grows, growing, grew, grown

**grower** *noun* growers

**guarantee\*** *noun* guarantees

**guarantee\*** *verb* guarantees, guaranteeing, guaranteed

**guard** *noun* guards

**guard** *verb* guards, guarding, guarded

**guess** *noun* guesses

**guess** *verb* guesses, guessing, guessed

**guest** *noun* guests

**guide** *noun* guides

**guide** *verb* guides, guiding, guided

**guilty** *adjective* guiltier, guiltiest

**guitar** *noun* guitars

**guitarist\*** *noun* guitarists

**gum** *noun* gums

**gun** *noun* guns

**gun** *verb* guns, gunning, gunned

**guy** *noun* guys

**gym** *noun* gyms

# Hh

**habit** *noun* habits

**hadn't**

This is short for *had not*. Put the apostrophe between the *n* and the *t*

**hair** *noun* hairs

**hairbrush** *noun* hairbrushes

**haircut** *noun* haircuts

**hairdresser** *noun* hairdressers

**hairdryer** *noun* hairdryers

**hairstyle** *noun* hairstyles

**half** *noun* halves

**hall** *noun* halls

**halve** *verb* halves, halving, halved

**ham** *noun* hams

**hamburger** *noun* hamburgers

**hand** *noun* hands

**hand** *verb* hands, handing, handed

**handbag** *noun* handbags

**handball** *noun* handballs

**handkerchief** *noun* handkerchiefs

**handle** *noun* handles

**handle** *verb* handles, handling, handled

**handsome** *adjective* handsomer, handsomest

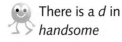 There is a *d* in *handsome*

**hang** *verb* hangs, hanging, hung or hanged

**happen** *verb* happens, happening, happened

**happy** *adjective* happier, happiest

**harass** *verb* harasses, harassing, harassed

**harbour** *noun* harbours

**harbour** *verb* harbours, harbouring, harboured

**hard** *adjective* harder, hardest

**hasn't**

This is short for *has not*. Put the apostrophe between the *n* and the *t*

**hat** *noun* hats

**hate** *noun* hates

**hate** *verb* hates, hating, hated

**have** *noun* haves

**have** *verb* has, having, had

**haven't**

This is short for *have not*. Put the apostrophe between the *n* and the *t*

**he** *pronoun*

**head** *noun* heads

**head** *verb* heads, heading, headed

**headache\*** *noun* headaches

**headline** *noun* headlines

**healthy** *adjective* healthier, healthiest

**hear** *verb* hears, hearing, heard

Do not confuse the spellings of *hear* and *here*: *I hear a dog barking; Come over here*

Do not confuse the spellings of *heard* and *herd*: *I thought I heard the phone; a herd of buffalo*

**heart** *noun* hearts

**heat** *verb* heats, heating, heated

**heater** *noun* heaters

**heavy** *adjective* heavier, heaviest

**he'd**

This is short for *he would* or *he had*. Put the apostrophe between the *e* and the *d*

**heel** *noun* heels

**heel** *verb* heels, heeling, heeled

**height\*** *noun* heights

**helicopter** *noun* helicopters

**he'll**

This is short for *he will*. Put the apostrophe between the *e* and the *l*

**hello** *noun* hellos

**help** *verb* helps, helping, helped

**herb** *noun* herbs

**herd** *noun* herds

**here** *adverb*

**he's**

This is short for *he is* or *he has*. Put the apostrophe between the *e* and the *s*

**hide** *noun* hides

**hide** *verb* hides, hiding, hid, hidden

**high** *adjective* higher, highest

**high** *noun* highs

**hill** *noun* hills

**hindrance** *noun* hindrances

**hire** *verb* hires, hiring, hired

**history** *noun* histories

**hit** *noun* hits

**hit** *verb* hits, hitting, hit

**hobby** *noun* hobbies

**hockey** *noun*

**hold** *noun* holds

**hold** *verb* holds, holding, held

**hole** *noun* holes

**hole** *verb* holes, holing, holed

Do not confuse the spellings of *hole* and *whole*: *You have a*

*hole in your sock; Emily was away for the whole of July*

**holiday** *noun* holidays

**holiday** *verb* holidays, holidaying, holidayed

**home** *noun* homes

**home** *verb* homes, homing, homed

Do not confuse the spellings of *home* and *hone*: *The police are homing in on a suspect; He spent hours honing his basketball skills*

**homicide\*** *noun* homicides

**hone** *verb* hones, honing, honed

**honey** *noun* honeys

**honeymoon** *noun* honeymoons

**hope** *noun* hopes

**hope** *verb* hopes, hoping, hoped

**hopeful** *adjective*

**horror** *noun* horrors

**horse** *noun* horses

**hospital** *noun* hospitals

**hostel** *noun* hostels

**hot** *adjective* hotter, hottest

**hotel** *noun* hotels

**hour** *noun* hours

**house** *noun* houses

**house** *verb* houses, housing, housed

**housewife** *noun* housewives

**how** *adverb*

**hug** *noun* hugs

**hug** *verb* hugs, hugging, hugged

**huge** *adjective* huger, hugest

**human** *noun* humans

**hundred** *noun* hundreds

**hundredth** *noun* hundredths

**hunger** *verb* hungers, hungering, hungered

**hungry** *adjective* hungrier, hungriest

**hunt** *noun* hunts

**hunt** *verb* hunts, hunting, hunted

**hurry** *verb* hurries, hurrying, hurried

**hurt** *verb* hurts, hurting, hurt

**husband** *noun* husbands

**hut** *noun* huts

**hyphen** *noun* hyphens

**hyphen** *verb* hyphens, hyphening, hyphened

# Ii

**I** *pronoun*

**ice** *noun* ices

**ice** *verb* ices, icing, iced

**icy** *adjective* icier, iciest

**ID** *noun* IDs

**I'd**

This is short for *I would* or *I had*. Put the apostrophe between the *I* and the *d*

**idea** *noun* ideas

**identification*** *noun* identifications

**identify** *verb* identifies, identifying, identified

**identity** *noun* identities

**if** *conjunction*

**ill** *noun* ills

**I'll**

This is short for *I will*. Put the apostrophe between the *I* and the first *l*

**illness** *noun* illnesses

**I'm**

This is short for *I am*. Put the apostrophe between the *I* and the *m*

**imagination** *noun* imaginations

**imagine** *verb* imagines, imagining, imagined

**immediately** *adverb*

**immigration** *noun*

**importance** *noun*

**important** *adjective*

**improve** *verb* improves, improving, improved

**improvement** *noun* improvements

**inbox** *noun* inboxes

**include** *verb* includes, including, included

**increase** *noun* increases

**increase** *verb* increases, increasing, increased

**independent** *adjective*

**individual*** *noun* individuals

**industry** *noun* industries

**infinitive*** *noun* infinitives

**inform** *verb* informs, informing, informed

**information*** *noun*

**ingredient** *noun* ingredients

**initial** *noun* initials

**initial** *verb* initials, initialling, initialled

**ink** *noun* inks

**inquiry** *noun* inquiries

**insect** *noun* insects

**inside** *noun* insides

**insist** *verb* insists, insisting, insisted

**installation** *noun* installations

**install** *verb* installs, installing, installed

**instance** *noun* instances

**instruction** *noun* instructions

**instructor** *noun* instructors

**instrument** *noun* instruments

**intend** *verb* intends, intending, intended

**interest** *noun* interests

**interest** *verb* interests, interesting, interested

**interfere** *verb* interferes, interfering, interfered

**intermediate*** *noun* intermediates

**international** *noun* internationals

**interrupt*** *noun* interrupts

**interrupt*** *verb* interrupts, interrupting, interrupted

**interval** *noun* intervals

**interview** *noun* interviews

**interview** *verb* interviews, interviewing, interviewed

**interviewer** *noun* interviewers

**introduce** *verb* introduces, introducing, introduced

**invent** *verb* invents, inventing, invented

**invention** *noun* inventions

**invitation** *noun* invitations

**invite** *verb* invites, inviting, invited

**involve** *verb* involves, involving, involved

**iron** *noun* irons

**iron** *verb* irons, ironing, ironed

**ironing** *noun*

**irregular*** *adjective*

**island** *noun* islands

**isn't**

This is short for *is not*. Put the apostrophe between the *n* and the *t*

**issue** *noun* issues

**issue** *verb* issues, issuing, issued

**it** *pronoun*

**item** *noun* items

**it'll**

This is short for *it will*. Put the apostrophe between the *t* and the first *l*

**its** *determiner*

**it's**

This is short for *it is*. Put the apostrophe between the *t* and the *s*. *It's going to be difficult to fit all this work in.*

Do not confuse with *its*. *Its* means 'belonging to it': *The dog wagged its tail.*

**I've**

This is short for *I have*. Put the apostrophe between the *I* and the *v*

# Jj

**jacket** *noun* jackets

**jail** *noun* jails

**jail** *verb* jails, jailing, jailed

**jam** *noun* jams

**jam** *verb* jams, jamming, jammed

**January** *noun*

**Japanese*** *adjective*

**jar** *noun* jars

**jar** *verb* jars, jarring, jarred

**jazz** *verb* jazzes, jazzing, jazzed

**jealous** *adjective*

**jet** *noun* jets

**jet** *verb* jets, jetting, jetted

**jewel** *noun* jewels

**jewellery*** *noun*

**job** *noun* jobs

**jog** *noun* jogs

**jog** *verb* jogs, jogging, jogged

**join** *noun* joins

**join** *verb* joins, joining, joined

**joke** *noun* jokes

**joke** *verb* jokes, joking, joked

**journalist** *noun* journalists

**journey** *noun* journeys

**journey** *verb* journeys, journeying, journeyed

**judge** *noun* judges

**judge** *verb* judges, judging, judged

**jug** *noun* jugs

**juice** *noun* juices

**juice** *verb* juices, juicing, juiced

**juicy** *adjective* juicier, juiciest

**July** *noun*

**jump** *noun* jumps

**jump** *verb* jumps, jumping, jumped

**jumper** *noun* jumpers

**June** *noun*

**jungle** *noun* jungles

# Kk

**kangaroo** *noun* kangaroos

**keen** *adjective* keener, keenest

**keen** *verb* keens, keening, keened

**keep** *noun* keeps

**keep** *verb* keeps, keeping, kept

Remember that the past tense of *keep* is *kept*

**key** *noun* keys

**key** *verb* keys, keying, keyed

**kg** *abbreviation* kgs

**kill** *verb* kills, killing, killed

**killer** *noun* killers

**kilo** *noun* kilos

**kilogram** *noun* kilograms

**kilometre\*** *noun* kilometres

**kind** *adjective* kinder, kindest

**kind** *noun* kinds

**king** *noun* kings

**kiss** *noun* kisses

**kiss** *verb* kisses, kissing, kissed

**kit** *noun* kits

**kit** *verb* kits, kitting, kitted

**kitchen** *noun* kitchens

**knee** *noun* knees

**knee** *verb* knees, kneeing, kneed

> Remember the silent *k*

**knife** *noun* knives

**knife** *verb* knifes, knifing, knifed

> Remember the silent *k*

**knock** *noun* knocks

**knock** *verb* knocks, knocking, knocked

> Remember the silent *k*

**know** *verb* knows, knowing, knew, known

> Do not confuse the spellings of *know* and *now*: I think I know that girl; Lunch is ready now

> Remember the silent *k*

**knowledge** *noun*

# Ll

**lab** *noun* labs

**label** *noun* labels

**label** *verb* labels, labelling, labelled

**laboratory\*** *noun* laboratories

**lack** *verb* lacks, lacking, lacked

**ladder** *noun* ladders

**lady** *noun* ladies

**lake** *noun* lakes

**lamb** *noun* lambs

**lamp** *noun* lamps

**land** *noun* lands

**land** *verb* lands, landing, landed

**lane** *noun* lanes

**language** *noun* languages

**large** *adjective* larger, largest

**last** *verb* lasts, lasting, lasted

**late** *adjective* later, latest

**laugh** *noun* laughs

**laugh** *verb* laughs, laughing, laughed

**law** *noun* laws

**lawyer** *noun* lawyers

**lay** *verb* lays, laying, laid

> Do not confuse *lay* with *lie*. *Lay* is a verb meaning 'to put something somewhere carefully', and must have an object: *Mothers often lay babies on their backs to sleep*. *Lie* is a verb meaning 'to be in a horizontal position': *I want to lie down*

**lazy** *adjective* lazier, laziest

**lead** *noun* leads

**lead** *verb* leads, leading, led

> Do not confuse the spellings of *lead* (the metal) and *led* (the past tense and past participle of the verb lead): *The pipes are made of lead; I led her through to the garden*

**leader** *noun* leaders

**leaf** *noun* leaves

**leaf** *verb* leafs, leafing, leafed

**league** *noun* leagues

**lean** *adjective* leaner, leanest

**lean** *verb* leans, leaning, leant or leaned

**learn** *verb* learns, learning, learned or learnt

**leather\*** *noun*

**leave** *verb* leaves, leaving, left

**lecture** *noun* lectures

**lecture** *verb* lectures, lecturing, lectured

**led** *verb*

Do not confuse the spellings of *led* (the past tense and past participle of the verb *lead*), and *lead* (the metal): *I led her through to the garden; The pipes are made of lead*

**left** *noun*

**left-click** *noun* left-clicks

**left-click** *verb* left-clicks, left-clicking, left-clicked

**leg** *noun* legs

**leisure*** *noun*

**lemon** *noun* lemons

**lemonade** *noun* lemonades

**lend** *verb* lends, lending, lent

**length** *noun* lengths

**lent** *verb*

Do not confuse the spellings of *lent* (the past tense and past participle of the verb *lend*) and *leant* (the past tense and past participle of the verb *lean*): *She lent me her bike; I leant against the wall*

**lesson** *noun* lessons

**let** *noun* lets

**let** *verb* lets, letting, let

**let's**

This is short for *let us*. Put the apostrophe between the *t* and the *s*

**letter** *noun* letters

**lettuce** *noun* lettuces

**level** *noun* levels

**level** *verb* levels, levelling, levelled

**library** *noun* libraries

**licence** *noun* licences

Do not confuse the spellings of the noun *licence* and the verb *license*: *a driving licence; Are you licensed to fly a plane?*

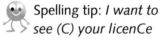 Spelling tip: *I want to see (C) your licenCe*

**license** *verb* licenses, licensing, licensed

**lid** *noun* lids

**lie** *verb* lies, lying, lay, lain

**lie** *verb* lies, lying, lied

Do not confuse *lie* with *lay*. There are two verbs written *lie*. When *lie* means 'to say something untruthful', the verb parts are *lies, lying* and *lied*. When *lie* means 'to be in a horizontal position', the verb parts are *lies, lying, lay* and *lain*

**life** *noun* lives

**lift** *noun* lifts

**lift** *verb* lifts, lifting, lifted

**light** *adjective* lighter, lightest

**light** *noun* lights

**light** *verb* lights, lighting, lighted, lit

**lighter** *noun* lighters

**lightning** *noun*

**like** *noun* likes

**like** *verb* likes, liking, liked

**likely** *adjective* likelier, likeliest

**limit** *noun* limits

**limit** *verb* limits, limiting, limited

**line** *noun* lines

**line** *verb* lines, lining, lined

**link** *noun* links

**link** *verb* links, linking, linked

**lion** *noun* lions

**lip** *noun* lips

**liquid** *noun* liquids

**list** *noun* lists

**list** *verb* lists, listing, listed

**listen** *verb* listens, listening, listened

**lit** *verb*

**litre*** *noun* litres

**live** *verb* lives, living, lived

**lively** *adjective* livelier, liveliest

**loan** *noun* loans

**loan** *verb* loans, loaning, loaned

**local** *noun* locals

**locate** *verb* locates, locating, located

**location** *noun* locations

**lock** *noun* locks

**lock** *verb* locks, locking, locked

**logo** *noun* logos

**lonely** *adjective* lonelier, loneliest

**long** *adjective* longer, longest

**long** *verb* longs, longing, longed

**look** *noun* looks

**look** *verb* looks, looking, looked

**loose** *adjective* looser, loosest

**loose** *verb* looses, loosing, loosed

The adjective and adverb *loose* is spelt with two *os*. Do not confuse it with the verb *lose*

**lorry** *noun* lorries

**lose** *verb* loses, losing, lost

Remember that the past tense of *lose* is *lost*

**lot** *noun* lots

Remember that *a lot* is written as two separate words

**lottery** *noun* lotteries

**loud** *adjective* louder, loudest

**love** *noun* loves

**love** *verb* loves, loving, loved

**lovely** *adjective* lovelier, loveliest

**lover** *noun* lovers

**low** *adjective* lower, lowest

**low** *noun* lows

**lower** *verb* lowers, lowering, lowered

**luck** *noun*

**lucky** *adjective* luckier, luckiest

**lunch** *noun* lunches

**lunch** *verb* lunches, lunching, lunched

**luxury** *noun* luxuries

# Mm

**machine** *noun* machines

**machine** *verb* machines, machining, machined

**mad** *adjective* madder, maddest

**madam** *noun* madams

**magazine** *noun* magazines

**magic** *noun*

**magician** *noun* magicians

**mail** *noun* mails

**mail** *verb* mails, mailing, mailed

**main** *adjective*

**make** *noun* makes

**make** *verb* makes, making, made

**make-up** *noun*

**male** *noun* males

**mall** *noun* malls

**man** *noun* men

**man** *verb* mans, manning, manned

**manage** *verb* manages, managing, managed

**manager** *noun* managers

**manageress** *noun* manageresses

**mango** *noun* mangoes or mangos

**map** *noun* maps

**map** *verb* maps, mapping, mapped

**March** *noun*

**march** *noun* marches

**march** *verb* marches, marching, marched

**mark** *noun* marks

**mark** *verb* marks, marking, marked

**market** *noun* markets

**market** *verb* markets, marketing, marketed

**marriage** *noun* marriages

**married** *adjective*

**marry** *verb* marries, marrying, married

**marvellous** *adjective*

**match** *noun* matches

**match** *verb* matches, matching, matched

**mate** *noun* mates

**mate** *verb* mates, mating, mated

**material** *noun* materials

**matter** *verb* matters, mattering, mattered

**maximum** *adjective*

**May** *noun*

**may** *verb*

**maybe** *adverb*

**meal** *noun* meals

**mean** *adjective* meaner, meanest

**mean** *noun* means

**mean** *verb* means, meaning, meant

**meaning** *noun* meanings

**meat** *noun* meats

**mechanic*** *noun* mechanics

**medical** *adjective*

**medicine** *noun* medicines

**medium** *noun* media or mediums

**meet** *verb* meets, meeting, met

Remember that the past tense of *meet* is *met*

**meeting** *noun* meetings

**melon** *noun* melons

**member** *noun* members

**membership** *noun* memberships

**memory** *noun* memories

**mend** *verb* mends, mending, mended

**mention** *noun* mentions

**mention** *verb* mentions, mentioning, mentioned

**menu** *noun* menus

**mess** *noun* messes

**mess** *verb* messes, messing, messed

**message** *noun* messages

**message** *verb* messages, messaging, messaged

**messy** *adjective* messier, messiest

**metal** *noun* metals

**meter** *noun* meters

**method** *noun* methods

**metre** *noun* metres

Do not confuse the spellings of *metre* and *meter*: *The wall is a metre high; the electricity meter*

**middle** *noun* middles

**mild** *adjective* milder, mildest

**mile** *noun* miles

**milk** *verb* milks, milking, milked

**millilitre** *noun* millilitres

**millimetre** *noun* millimetres

**million** *noun* millions

**millionth** *noun* millionths

**mind** *noun* minds

**mind** *verb* minds, minding, minded

**mine** *noun* mines

**mine** *verb* mines, mining, mined

**minimum** *adjective*

**minus** *adjective*

**minute** *noun* minutes

**minute** *verb* minutes, minuting, minuted

**mirror** *noun* mirrors

**mirror** *verb* mirrors, mirroring, mirrored

**mischief** *noun*

**mischievous*** *adjective*

**Miss** *noun* Misses

**miss** *noun* misses

**miss** *verb* misses, missing, missed

**mistake** *noun* mistakes

**mistake** *verb* mistakes, mistaking, mistook, mistaken

**mix** *noun* mixes

**mix** *verb* mixes, mixing, mixed

**mixture** *noun* mixtures

**mobile** *noun* mobiles

**model** *noun* models

**model** *verb* models, modelling, modelled

**modern** *adjective*

**moment** *noun* moments

**Monday** *noun* Mondays

**money** *noun*

**monkey** *noun* monkeys

**monster** *noun* monsters

**month** *noun* months

**monthly** *adjective*

**monument** *noun* monuments

**mood** *noun* moods

**moon** *noun* moons

**morning** *noun* mornings

> Do not confuse the spellings of *morning* and *mourning*: *a sunny morning; a week of national mourning*

**mosquito*** *noun* mosquitoes or mosquitos

**mother** *noun* mothers

**mother** *verb* mothers, mothering, mothered

**motorbike** *noun* motorbikes

**motorway** *noun* motorways

**mountain** *noun* mountains

**mourning** *noun*

**mouse** *noun* mice

**moustache** *noun* moustaches

**mouth** *noun* mouths

**mouth** *verb* mouths, mouthing, mouthed

**move** *noun* moves

**move** *verb* moves, moving, moved

**movie** *noun* movies

**Mr** *noun*

**Mrs** *noun*

**Ms** *noun*

**mug** *noun* mugs

**mug** *verb* mugs, mugging, mugged

**mum** *noun* mums

**mummy** *noun* mummies

**murder** *noun* murders

**murder** *verb* murders, murdering, murdered

**murderer** *noun* murderers

**muscle** *noun* muscles

**muscle** *verb* muscles, muscling, muscled

**museum** *noun* museums

**mushroom** *noun* mushrooms

**mushroom** *verb* mushrooms, mushrooming, mushroomed

**musical** *noun* musicals

**musician** *noun* musicians

**must** *verb*

**mysterious*** *adjective*

**mystery*** *noun* mysteries

# Nn

**name** *noun* names

**name** *verb* names, naming, named

**narrow** *adjective* narrower, narrowest

**narrow** *verb* narrows, narrowing, narrowed

**nasty** *adjective* nastier, nastiest

**national** *noun* nationals

**nationality** *noun* nationalities

**natural** *noun* naturals

**nature** *noun* natures

**naughty** *adjective* naughtier, naughtiest

**near** *adjective* nearer, nearest

**near** *verb* nears, nearing, neared

**neat** *adjective* neater, neatest

**necessary** *adjective*

**necessity** *noun* necessities

**neck** *noun* necks

**necklace** *noun* necklaces

**need** *noun* needs

**need** *verb* needs, needing, needed

**negative** *noun* negatives

**neighbour\*** *noun* neighbours

**neighbour\*** *verb* neighbours, neighbouring, neighboured

**neighbourhood\*** *noun* neighbourhoods

**nephew** *noun* nephews

**nervous** *adjective*

**net** *noun* nets

**new** *adjective* newer, newest

**newspaper** *noun* newspapers

**nice** *adjective* nicer, nicest

**niece** *noun* nieces

**night** *noun* nights

**nightlife** *noun*

**nightmare** *noun* nightmares

**nine** *noun* nines

**nineteen** *noun* nineteens

**nineteenth** *noun* nineteenths

**ninetieth** *noun* ninetieths

**ninety** *noun* nineties

**ninth** *noun* ninths

**no** *interjection, determiner, adverb*

**nobody** *noun* nobodies

**noise** *noun* noises

**noisy** *adjective* noisier, noisiest

**none** *pronoun*

> Do not confuse *none* with *nun*: None of my friends are here yet; an order of Italian nuns

**noodle** *noun* noodles

**noon** *noun* noons

**north** *noun*

**nose** *noun* noses

**nose** *verb* noses, nosing, nosed

**not** *adverb*

**note** *noun* notes

**note** *verb* notes, noting, noted

**notebook** *noun* notebooks

**nothing** *noun* nothings

**notice** *noun* notices

**notice** *verb* notices, noticing, noticed

**noticeboard** *noun* noticeboards

**noun** *noun* nouns

**novel** *noun* novels

**November** *noun*

**now** *adverb*

> Do not confuse the spellings of *now* and *know*: Lunch is ready now; I think I know that girl

**nuisance\*** *noun* nuisances

**number** *noun* numbers

**number** *verb* numbers, numbering, numbered

**nun** *noun* nuns

> Do not confuse *nun* with *none*: an order of Italian nuns; None of my friends are here yet

**nurse** *noun* nurses

**nurse** *verb* nurses, nursing, nursed

# Oo

**object** *noun* objects

**object** *verb* objects, objecting, objected

**occasion\*** *noun* occasions

**occasionally\*** *adverb*

**occupation** *noun* occupations

**occupy** *verb* occupies, occupying, occupied

**occur** *verb* occurs, occurring, occurred

**occurrence** *noun* occurrences

**ocean** *noun* oceans

**October** *noun*

**of** *preposition*

> Do not confuse the spellings of *of* and *off*: a bunch of tulips; Do you want to take off your coat?

**off** *preposition, adverb, adjective*

**offer** *noun* offers

**offer** *verb* offers, offering, offered

**office** *noun* offices

**officer** *noun* officers

**often** *adverb*

**oil** *noun* oils

**oil** *verb* oils, oiling, oiled

**okay** *noun* okays

**okay** *verb* okays, okaying, okayed

**old** *adjective* older, oldest

**older** *adjective*

Do not confuse *older* and *elder*. *Older* simply means 'more old', and can be used of people or things, and can be followed by *than*: *My car is older than yours.* *Elder* is used when you are saying which of two people was born first. It is not used with *than*: *I live with my elder sister; He is the elder of the two.*

**old-fashioned** *adjective*

**olive** *noun* olives

**omelette*** *noun* omelettes

**one** *noun* ones

Do not confuse the spellings of *one* and *won*. *One* is a number. *Won* is the past tense of *win*

**onion** *noun* onions

**open** *adjective*

**open** *verb* opens, opening, opened

**opera** *noun* operas

**operate** *verb* operates, operating, operated

**operation** *noun* operations

**opinion** *noun* opinions

**opportunity*** *noun* opportunities

**opposite** *noun* opposites

**option** *noun* options

**orange** *noun* oranges

**orchestra*** *noun* orchestras

**order** *noun* orders

**order** *verb* orders, ordering, ordered

**ordinary** *adjective*

**organization*** *noun* organizations

This noun can also be spelled with *isation*

**organize** *verb* organizes, organizing, organized

This verb can also be spelt with *ise*

**original** *noun* originals

**other** *noun* others

**ought** *verb*

**our** *determiner*

Do not confuse *our* and *are*, which some people pronounce the same way

**out** *adverb*

**outside** *noun* outsides

**oven** *noun* ovens

**over** *preposition, adverb*

**overnight** *adverb, adjective*

**owe** *verb* owes, owing, owed

**own** *verb* owns, owning, owned

**owner** *noun* owners

# Pp

**pack** *noun* packs

**pack** *verb* packs, packing, packed

**package** *noun* packages, packaging, packaged

**packet** *noun* packets

**page** *noun* pages

**page** *verb* pages, paging, paged

**pail** *noun* pails

Do not confuse the spellings of *pail* and *pale*. A *pail* is a bucket. *Pale* means very light in colour

**pain** *noun* pains

Do not confuse the spellings of *pain* and *pane*. A *pain* is a feeling caused by disease or injury. A *pane* is a piece of glass in a window

**pain** *verb* pains, paining, pained

**paint** *noun* paints

**paint** *verb* paints, painting, painted

**painter** *noun* painters

**painting** *noun* paintings

**pair** *noun* pairs

**pair** *verb* pairs, pairing, paired

Do note confuse the spellings of *pair* and *pear*. A *pair* is a set of two things. A *pear* is a fruit

**palace** *noun* palaces

**pale** *adjective* paler, palest

**pan** *noun* pans

**pan** *verb* pans, panning, panned

**pane** *noun* panes

**paper** *noun* papers

**paper** *verb* papers, papering, papered

**paragraph*** *noun* paragraphs

**parcel** *noun* parcels

**parcel** *verb* parcels, parcelling, parcelled

**parent** *noun* parents

**park** *noun* parks

**park** *verb* parks, parking, parked

**parliament*** *noun* parliaments

**parrot** *noun* parrots

**part** *noun* parts

**part** *verb* parts, parting, parted

**particular** *noun* particulars

**partner** *noun* partners

**partner** *verb* partners, partnering, partnered

**party** *noun* parties

**pass** *noun* passes

**pass** *verb* passes, passing, passed

Do not confuse the spellings of *passed* and *past*: We passed an accident on the way here; Go past the garage and turn left

**passenger** *noun* passengers

**passive** *adjective*

**passport** *noun* passports

**password** *noun* passwords

**past** *preposition, adverb*

**pasta** *noun* pastas

**path** *noun* paths

**patient** *noun* patients

**pattern** *noun* patterns

**pause** *noun* pauses

**pause** *verb* pauses, pausing, paused

**pavement** *noun* pavements

**pay** *verb* pays, paying, paid

**pea** *noun* peas

**peace** *noun*

Do not confuse the spellings of *peace* and *piece*: I love the peace and quiet here; a piece of cheese

**peach** *noun* peaches

**peak** *noun* peaks

**peak** *verb* peaks, peaking, peaked

**peanut** *noun* peanuts

**pear** *noun* pears

Do note confuse the spellings of *pear* and *pair*. A *pear* is a fruit. A *pair* is a set of two things

**peculiar** *adjective*

**pedestrian*** *noun* pedestrians

**pen** *noun* pens

**pen** *verb* pens, penning, penned

**pencil** *noun* pencils

**penguin** *noun* penguins

**penny** *noun* pennies or pence

**people** *noun* peoples

**people** *verb* peoples, peopling, peopled

**pepper** *noun* peppers

**perfect** *noun* perfects

**perfect** *verb* perfects, perfecting, perfected

**perform** *verb* performs, performing, performed

**performance*** *noun*
performances

**perfume** *noun* perfumes

**perfume** *verb* perfumes,
perfuming, perfumed

**perhaps** *adverb*

**period** *noun* periods

**permission*** *noun*
permissions

**permit** *noun* permits

**permit** *verb* permits,
permitting, permitted

**person** *noun* people or
persons

**personal*** *adjective*

**persuade** *verb* persuades,
persuading, persuaded

**pet** *noun* pets

**pet** *verb* pets, petting,
petted

**pharmacy*** *noun*
pharmacies

**phone** *noun* phones

**phone** *verb* phones,
phoning, phoned

**photo** *noun* photos

**photocopy** *noun*
photocopies

**photocopy** *verb*
photocopies, photocopying,
photocopied

**photograph*** *noun*
photographs

**photograph*** *verb*
photographs,

photographing,
photographed

**photographer*** *noun*
photographers

**phrase** *noun* phrases

**phrase** *verb* phrases,
phrasing, phrased

**physical*** *adjective*

**piano** *noun* pianos

**pick** *noun* picks

**pick** *verb* picks, picking,
picked

**picnic** *noun* picnics

**picnic** *verb* picnics,
picnicking, picnicked

**picture** *noun* pictures

**picture** *verb* pictures,
picturing, pictured

**pie** *noun* pies

**piece** *noun* pieces

**piece** *verb* pieces, piecing,
pieced

> Spelling tip: *have a
> pIEce of pIE*

> Do not confuse the
> spellings of *piece* and
> *peace*: *a piece of
> cheese; I love the peace
> and quiet here*

**pig** *noun* pigs

**pile** *noun* piles

**pile** *verb* piles, piling, piled

**pill** *noun* pills

**pillow** *noun* pillows

**pilot** *noun* pilots

**pilot** *verb* pilots, piloting,
piloted

**pin** *noun* pins

**pin** *verb* pins, pinning,
pinned

**pineapple*** *noun*
pineapples

**pink** *noun* pinks

**pink** *adjective* pinker,
pinkest

**pipe** *noun* pipes

**pipe** *verb* pipes, piping,
piped

**pirate** *noun* pirates

**pity** *verb* pities, pitying,
pitied

**pizza** *noun* pizzas

**place** *noun* places

**place** *verb* places, placing,
placed

**plain** *adjective* plainer,
plainest

**plain** *noun* plains

> Do not confuse the
> spellings of *plain* and
> *plane*: *lions who live
> on the African plains; If
> you don't hurry up you
> will miss your plane*

**plan** *noun* plans

**plan** *verb* plans, planning,
planned

**plane** *noun* planes

**plane** *verb* planes, planing,
planed

**planet** *noun* planets

**plant** *noun* plants

**plant** *verb* plants, planting, planted

**plastic** *noun* plastics

**plate** *noun* plates

**platform** *noun* platforms

**play** *noun* plays

**play** *verb* plays, playing, played

**player** *noun* players

**playground** *noun* playgrounds

**please** *verb* pleases, pleasing, pleased

**pleasure** *noun* pleasures

**plenty** *noun*

**plug** *noun* plugs

**plug** *verb* plugs, plugging, plugged

**plural** *noun* plurals

**plus** *adjective*

**pocket** *noun* pockets

**pocket** *verb* pockets, pocketing, pocketed

**poem** *noun* poems

**poet** *noun* poets

**point** *noun* points

**point** *verb* points, pointing, pointed

**police** *verb* polices, policing, policed

**policeman** *noun* policemen

**policewoman** *noun* policewomen

**politician*** *noun* politicians

**pollution** *noun*

**pool** *noun* pools

**pool** *verb* pools, pooling, pooled

**poor** *adjective* poorer, poorest

**pop** *noun* pops

**pop** *verb* pops, popping, popped

**popular*** *adjective*

**population** *noun* populations

**pore** *noun* pores

**pore** *verb* pores, poring, pored

**port** *noun* ports

**position** *noun* positions

**position** *verb* positions, positioning, positioned

**positive** *noun* positives

**possession** *noun* possessions

**possessive*** *noun* possessives

**possibility*** *noun* possibilities

**possible** *adjective*

**post** *noun* posts

**post** *verb* posts, posting, posted

**poster** *noun* posters

**postman** *noun* postmen

**postpone*** *verb* postpones, postponing, postponed

**pot** *noun* pots

**pot** *verb* pots, potting, potted

**potato** *noun* potatoes

**pound** *noun* pounds

**pound** *verb* pounds, pounding, pounded

**pour** *verb* pours, pouring, poured

Do not confuse the spellings of *pour* and *pore*: *The rain was pouring down the window; Aila was poring over a book*

**powder** *noun* powders

**powder** *verb* powders, powdering, powdered

**power** *noun* powers

**power** *verb* powers, powering, powered

**practice** *noun* practices

Do not confuse the spellings of the noun *practice* and the verb *practise*: *You won't get better without practice; I practise the piano every day*

Spelling tip: *I went to see (C) the doctor's new practiCe*

**practise** *verb* practises, practising, practised

Spelling tip: *you must practiSe your Spelling*

**pray** *verb* prays, praying, prayed

Do not confuse the spellings of *pray* and *prey*: *Muslims pray five times a day; Owls prey on mice and small birds*

**prayer** *noun* prayers

**predict** *verb* predicts, predicting, predicted

**prefer** *verb* prefers, preferring, preferred

**prejudice*** *noun* prejudices

**preparation** *noun* preparations

**prepare** *verb* prepare, preparing, prepared

**preposition*** *noun* prepositions

**present** *noun* presents

**present** *verb* presents, presenting, presented

**presentation** *noun* presentations

**president** *noun* presidents

**press** *verb* presses, pressing, pressed

**pressure** *noun* pressures

**pretty** *adjective* prettier, prettiest

**prevent** *verb* prevents, preventing, prevented

**prey** *verb* preys, preying, preyed

**price** *noun* prices

**price** *verb* prices, pricing, priced

Do not confuse *price* with *prize*. The *price* of something is the amount of money you pay to buy it: *The price of a cup of coffee is £2*. A *prize* is something given to someone for winning a competition: *He won first prize in a music competition*

**priest** *noun* priests

**primary** *noun* primaries

**prince** *noun* princes

**princess** *noun* princesses

**principal** *noun* principals

Do not confuse the spellings of *principal* and *principle*: *the principal reason; the school principal; Eating meat is against my principles*

Spelling tip: *pAL up with the principAL and principAL teachers*

**principle** *noun* principles

**print** *noun* prints

**print** *verb* prints, printing, printed

**printer** *noun* printers

**printing** *noun* printings

**printout** *noun* printouts

**prise** *verb* prises, prising, prised

Do not confuse the spellings of *prise* and *prize*: *A prisoner had prised the wire fence apart; Analytical skills are highly prized in business*

**prison** *noun* prisons

**prisoner** *noun* prisoners

**private** *noun* privates

**privilege*** *noun* privileges

**prize** *verb* prizes, prizing, prized

**probably** *adverb*

**problem** *noun* problems

**produce** *verb* produces, producing, produced

**product** *noun* products

**profession*** *noun* professions

**professional*** *noun* professionals

**professor*** *noun* professors

**program** *noun* programs

**program** *verb* programs, programming, programmed

Do not confuse *program* with *programme*. You *program* a computer but you watch a television *programme*.

135

**programme** *noun* programmes

**progress** *verb* progresses, progressing, progressed

**project** *noun* projects

**project** *verb* projects, projecting, projected

**promise** *noun* promises

**promise** *verb* promises, promising, promised

**promote** *verb* promotes, promoting, promoted

**pronoun** *noun* pronouns

**pronounce** *verb* pronounces, pronouncing, pronounced

> There is an *o* before the *u* in *pronounce*

**pronunciation*** *noun* pronunciations

> There is no *o* before the *u* in *pronunciation*

**property** *noun* properties

**protect** *verb* protects, protecting, protected

**proud** *adjective* prouder, proudest

**prove** *verb* proves, proving, proved or proven

**provide** *verb* provides, providing, provided

**provider** *noun* providers

**pub** *noun* pubs

**publish** *verb* publishes, publishing, published

**pull** *noun* pulls

**pull** *verb* pulls, pulling, pulled

**pullover** *noun* pullovers

**pump** *noun* pumps

**pump** *verb* pumps, pumping, pumped

**pumpkin** *noun* pumpkins

**punctuation*** *noun* punctuations

**punish** *verb* punishes, punishing, punished

**pup** *noun* pups

**pupil** *noun* pupils

**puppy** *noun* puppies

**pure** *adjective* purer, purest

**purple** *adjective*

**purpose** *noun* purposes

**purse** *noun* purses

**purse** *verb* purses, pursing, pursed

**push** *noun* pushes

**push** *verb* pushes, pushing, pushed

**put** *verb* puts, putting, put

> Remember that the past tense of *put* is *put*

**puzzle** *noun* puzzles

**puzzle** *verb* puzzles, puzzling, puzzled

# Qq

**qualification*** *noun* qualifications

**quality** *noun* qualities

**quantity** *noun* quantities

**quarter** *noun* quarters

**quarter** *verb* quarters, quartering, quartered

**queen** *noun* queens

**question** *noun* questions

**question** *verb* questions, questioning, questioned

**questionnaire*** *noun* questionnaires

**queue** *noun* queues

**queue** *verb* queues, queueing, queuing or queued

> Do not confuse the spellings of *queue* and *cue*: *a long queue at the bank; That's the lead singer's cue*

**quick** *adjective* quicker, quickest

**quiet** *adjective* quieter, quietest

**quiet** *verb* quiets, quieting, quieted

> Do not confuse the spellings of *quiet* and the adverb *quite*

**quilt** *noun* quilts

**quilt** *verb* quilts, quilting, quilted

**quit** *verb* quits, quitting, quit

**quite** *adverb*

**quiz** *noun* quizzes

**quiz** *verb* quizzes, quizzing, quizzed

# Rr

**rabbit** *noun* rabbits

**race** *noun* races

**race** *verb* races, racing, raced

**racket** *noun* rackets

**radio** *noun* radios

**radio** *verb* radios, radioing, radioed

**rail** *noun* rails

**railway** *noun* railways

**rain** *noun* rains

**rain** *verb* rains, raining, rained

>  Do not confuse the spellings of *rain*, *rein* and *reign*: *The rain has finally stopped; Pull the reins sharply if you want to turn; the reign of King John*

**raincoat** *noun* raincoats

**raindrop** *noun* raindrops

**rainforest** *noun* rainforests

**rainstorm** *noun* rainstorms

**rainy** *adjective* rainier, rainiest

**raise** *verb* raises, raising, raised

> Do not confuse *raise* with *rise*. *Raise* is a verb that takes an object: *He raised his cup to his lips*. *Rise* is a verb that does not take an object: *Columns of smoke rose into the sky*

**range** *noun* ranges

**range** *verb* ranges, ranging, ranged

**rap** *noun* raps

**rap** *verb* raps, rapping, rapped

> Do not confuse the spellings of *rap* and *wrap*: *The teacher rapped the table with a ruler; I have wrapped all my Christmas presents*

**rare** *adjective* rarer, rarest

**raspberry\*** *noun* raspberries

**rat** *noun* rats

**reach** *verb* reaches, reaching, reached

**read** *verb* reads, reading, read

> Remember that the past tense of *read* has the same spelling but rhymes with *bed*

**reader** *noun* readers

**reading** *noun* readings

**ready** *adjective* readier, readiest

**real** *adjective*

**realize** *verb* realizes, realizing, realized

> This verb can also be spelt with *ise*

**really** *adverb*

**reason** *noun* reasons

**reason** *verb* reasons, reasoning, reasoned

**rebuild** *verb* rebuilds, rebuilding, rebuilt

**receipt** *noun* receipts

**receive** *verb* receives, receiving, received

**recent** *adjective*

**reception** *noun* receptions

**receptionist** *noun* receptionists

**recipe** *noun* recipes

**recognize** *verb* recognizes, recognizing, recognized

> This verb can also be spelt with *ise*

**recommend** *verb* recommends, recommending, recommended

**record** *noun* records

**record** *verb* records, recording, recorded

**recording** *noun* recordings

**recover** *verb* recovers, recovering, recovered

**recycle** *verb* recycles, recycling, recycled

**recycling** *noun*

**red** *adjective* redder, reddest

**red** *noun* reds

**reduce** *verb* reduces, reducing, reduced

**refreshment** *noun* refreshments

**refund** *noun* refunds

**refund** *verb* refunds, refunding, refunded

**refuse** *verb* refuses, refusing, refused

**regard** *verb* regards, regarding, regarded

**region** *noun* regions

**register** *noun* registers

**register** *verb* registers, registering, registered

**registration** *noun* registrations

**regret** *noun* regrets

**regret** *verb* regrets, regretting, regretted

**regular** *noun* regulars

**reign\*** *noun* reigns

**reign\*** *verb* reigns, reigning, reigned

**relation** *noun* relations

**relationship\*** *noun* relationships

**relative** *noun* relatives

**relax** *verb* relaxes, relaxing, relaxed

**relevant** *adjective*

**religion** *noun* religions

**religious** *adjective*

**remember** *verb* remembers, remembering, remembered

**remind** *verb* reminds, reminding, reminded

**remove** *verb* removes, removing, removed

**rent** *noun* rents

**rent** *verb* rents, renting, rented

**repair** *noun* repairs

**repair** *verb* repairs, repairing, repaired

**repeat** *noun* repeats

**repeat** *verb* repeats, repeating, repeated

**replace** *verb* replaces, replacing, replaced

**reply** *noun* replies

**reply** *verb* replies, replying, replied

**report** *noun* reports

**report** *verb* reports, reporting, reported

**reporter** *noun* reporters

**request** *noun* requests

**request** *verb* requests, requesting, requested

**require** *verb* requires, requiring, required

**rescue** *noun* rescues

**rescue** *verb* rescues, rescuing, rescued

**research** *verb* researches, researching, researched

**resell** *verb* resells, reselling, resold

**reservation\*** *noun* reservations

**reserve** *noun* reserves

**reserve** *verb* reserves, reserving, reserved

**resort** *noun* resorts

**resort** *verb* resorts, resorting, resorted

**respect** *noun* respects

**respect** *verb* respects, respecting, respected

**rest** *noun* rests

**rest** *verb* rests, resting, rested

**restaurant\*** *noun* restaurants

**result** *noun* results

**result** *verb* results, resulting, resulted

**retire** *verb* retires, retiring, retired

**return** *noun* returns

**return** *verb* returns, returning, returned

**review\*** *noun* reviews

**review\*** *verb* reviews, reviewing, reviewed

**revise** *verb* revises, revising, revised

**revision** *noun* revisions

**reward** *noun* rewards

**reward** *verb* rewards, rewarding, rewarded

**rhyme\*** *noun* rhymes

**rhythm\*** *noun* rhythms

**rice** *noun*

**rich** *adjective* richer, richest

**riches** *plural* noun

**ride** *noun* rides

**ride** *verb* rides, riding, rode, ridden

> Remember that the past tense of *ride* is *rode* and the past participle is *ridden*

**rider** *noun* riders

**right** *noun* rights

**right** *verb* rights, righting, righted

> Do not confuse the spellings of *right*, *write* and *rite*: Is that the right answer?; Write your name on the jotter; the marriage rites of the Christian Church

**right-click** *noun* right-clicks

**right-click** *verb* right-clicks, right-clicking, right-clicked

**ring** *noun* rings

**ring** *verb* rings, ringing, rang, rung

**ring** *verb* rings, ringing, ringed

> When *ring* means 'to make a sound like a bell', the past tense is *rang* and the past participle is *rung*. When *ring* means 'to surround', the past tense and past participle is *ringed*

**rise** *verb* rises, rising, rose, risen

> Do not confuse *rise* and *arise*. When someone or something *rises*, they move upward: *He rose to greet her. Rise* also means to increase: *prices have risen*. When an opportunity or problem *arises*, it begins to exist: *A difficulty has arisen*
>
> Do not confuse *rise* with *raise. Rise* is a verb that does not take an object: *Columns of smoke rose into the sky. Raise* is a verb that takes an object: *He raised the cup to his lips*

**rite** *noun* rites

**river** *noun* rivers

**road** *noun* roads

**roast** *noun* roasts

**roast** *verb* roasts, roasting, roasted

**rob** *verb* robs, robbing, robbed

**robot** *noun* robots

**rock** *noun* rocks

**rock** *verb* rocks, rocking, rocked

**rode** *verb*

**role** *noun* roles

> Do not confuse the spellings of *role* and *roll*: He has won a leading role in a musical; We need another roll of wallpaper

**roll** *noun* rolls

**roll** *verb* rolls, rolling, rolled

**romance** *noun* romances

**romantic** *noun* romantics

**roof** *noun* roofs

**roof** *verb* roofs, roofing, roofed

**room** *noun* rooms

**root** *noun* roots

> Do not confuse the spellings of *root* and *route*. A *root* is the part of a plant that grows beneath the soil. The *route* is the way you get to a place

**root** *verb* roots, rooting, rooted

**rose** *noun* roses

**rough** *adjective* rougher, roughest

**rough** *noun* roughs

**round** *adjective* rounder, roundest

**round** *noun* rounds

**round** *verb* rounds, rounding, rounded

**roundabout** *noun* roundabouts

**route** *noun* routes

**routine** *noun* routines

**row** *noun* rows

**row** *verb* rows, rowing, rowed

> Do not confuse the different ways of pronouncing *row*. A *row* is an argument and rhymes with *cow*. A *row* is a line of things and rhymes with *go*. To *row* means to make a boat move by using oars and rhymes with *go*.

**rubber** *noun* rubbers

**rubbish** *verb* rubbishes, rubbishing, rubbished

**rude** *adjective* ruder, rudest

**rug** *noun* rugs

**ruin** *noun* ruins

**ruin** *verb* ruins, ruining, ruined

**rule** *noun* rules

**rule** *verb* rules, ruling, ruled

**ruler** *noun* rulers

**run** *noun* runs

**run** *verb* runs, running, ran, run

**rung** *noun* rungs

**runner** *noun* runners

**Russian** *noun* Russians

# Ss

**sacrifice*** *noun* sacrifices

**sacrifice*** *verb* sacrifices, sacrificing, sacrificed

**sad** *adjective* sadder, saddest

**safe** *adjective* safer, safest

**safe** *noun* safes

**sail** *noun* sails

**sail** *verb* sails, sailing, sailed

> Do not confuse *sail* (a large sheet that catches the wind to make a boat go) and *sale* (the selling of goods for money)

**sailing** *noun* sailings

**sailor** *noun* sailors

**salad** *noun* salads

**salary** *noun* salaries

**sale** *noun* sales

**salesman** *noun* salesmen

**saleswoman** *noun* saleswomen

**salmon** *noun* salmons or salmon

**salon** *noun* salons

**salt** *noun* salts

**salt** *verb* salts, salting, salted

**sand** *noun* sands

**sand** *verb* sands, sanding, sanded

**sandal** *noun* sandals

**sandwich** *noun* sandwiches

**sandwich** *verb* sandwiches, sandwiching, sandwiched

> Spelling tip: there's SAND in my SANDwich

**sandy** *adjective* sandier, sandiest

**Saturday** *noun* Saturdays

**sauce** *noun* sauces

> Do not confuse the spellings of *sauce* and *source*, which can sound very similar in some accents

**saucepan** *noun* saucepans

**saucer** *noun* saucers

**sausage** *noun* sausages

**save** *noun* saves

**save** *verb* saves, saving, saved

**savoury*** *adjective*

**saw** *noun* saws

**saw** *verb* saws, sawing, sawed, sawn

**say** *verb* says, saying, said

> Remember that the past tense of *say* is spelt *said* and pronounced 'sed'

**scarf** *noun* scarfs or scarves

**scary** *adjective* scarier, scariest

**scene** *noun* scenes

**scenery** *noun*

**scent** *noun* scents

**schedule*** *noun* schedules

**schedule*** *verb* schedules, scheduling, scheduled

**school** *noun* schools

**school** *verb* schools, schooling, schooled

**schoolboy** *noun* schoolboys

**schoolchild** *noun* schoolchildren

**schoolgirl** *noun* schoolgirls

**schoolmate** *noun* schoolmates

**schoolroom** *noun* schoolrooms

**schoolteacher** *noun* schoolteachers

**science** *noun* sciences

**scientist** *noun* scientists

**scooter** *noun* scooters

**score** *noun* scores

**score** *verb* scores, scoring, scored

**scorer** *noun* scorers

**scream** *noun* screams

**scream** *verb* screams, screaming, screamed

**screen** *noun* screens

**screen** *verb* screens, screening, screened

**sculpture** *noun* sculptures

**sea** *noun* seas

> Do not confuse *sea* with *see*. The *sea* is a large area of salt water. If you *see* something, you look at it

**search** *noun* searches

**search** *verb* searches, searching, searched

**season** *noun* seasons

**season** *verb* seasons, seasoning, seasoned

**seat** *noun* seats

**seat** *verb* seats, seating, seated

**second** *noun* seconds

**second** *verb* seconds, seconding, seconded

**secondary** *noun* secondaries

**secret** *noun* secrets

**secretary*** *noun* secretaries

**section** *noun* sections

**security*** *noun* securities

**see** *verb* sees, seeing, saw, seen

> Remember that the past tense of *see* is *saw*

**seem** *verb* seems, seeming, seemed

**select** *verb* selects, selecting, selected

**sell** *verb* sells, selling, sold

> Remember that the past tense of *sell* is *sold*

**seller** *noun* sellers

**send** *verb* sends, sending, sent

> Do not confuse the spellings of *sent* (the past tense and past participle of *send*) and *scent* (a nice smell): *I sent Anna a birthday card; the scent of lilies*

**sense** *noun* senses

**sense** *verb* senses, sensing, sensed

**sensible** *adjective*

**sentence** *noun* sentences

**sentence** *verb* sentences, sentencing, sentenced

**separate*** *verb* separates, separating, separated

**September** *noun*

**series** *noun* series

**serial** *noun* serials

> Do not confuse the spellings of *serial* and *cereal*: *a new drama serial; my favourite breakfast cereal*

**serve** *verb* serves, serving, served

**server** *noun* servers

**service** *noun* services

**service** *verb* services, servicing, serviced

**session** *noun* sessions

**set** *noun* sets

**set** *verb* sets, setting, set

**seven** *noun* sevens

**seventeen** *noun* seventeens

**seventeenth** *noun* seventeenths

**seventh** *noun* sevenths

**seventieth** *noun* seventieths

**seventy** *noun* seventies

**sew** *verb* sews, sewing, sewed, sewn

> Do not confuse *sew* with *sow*. To *sew* is to work with a thread and needle. To *sow* is to put seed into the ground

**sex** *noun* sexes

**shade** *noun* shades

**shade** *verb* shades, shading, shaded

**shadow** *noun* shadows

**shadow** *verb* shadows, shadowing, shadowed

**shake** *verb* shakes, shaking, shook, shaken

**shame** *noun* shames

**shame** *verb* shames, shaming, shamed

**shampoo** *noun* shampoos

**shampoo** *verb* shampoos, shampooing, shampooed

**shape** *noun* shapes

**shape** *verb* shapes, shaping, shaped

**share** *noun* shares

**share** *verb* shares, sharing, shared

**shark** *noun* sharks

**sharp** *adjective* sharper, sharpest

**sharp** *noun* sharps

**shave** *verb* shaves, shaving, shaved

**shaven** *adjective*

**she'd**

> This is short for *she would* or *she had*. Put the apostrophe between the *e* and the *d*

**sheep** *noun* sheep

**sheet** *noun* sheets

**shelf** *noun* shelves

**she'll**

> This is short for *she will*. Put the apostrophe between the *e* and the first *l*

**she's**

> This is short for *she is* or *she has*. Put the apostrophe between the *e* and the *s*

**shine** *verb* shines, shining, shone

**shiny** *adjective* shinier, shiniest

**ship** *noun* ships

**ship** *verb* ships, shipping, shipped

**shirt** *noun* shirts

**shock** *noun* shocks

**shock** *verb* shocks, shocking, shocked

**shoe** *noun* shoes

**shook** *verb*

**shoot** *noun* shoots

**shoot** *verb* shoots, shooting, shot

**shop** *noun* shops

**shop** *verb* shops, shopping, shopped

**shore** *noun* shores

**shore** *verb* shores, shoring, shored

**short** *adjective* shorter, shortest

**shot** *noun* shots

**should** *verb*

**shoulder** *noun* shoulders

**shoulder** *verb* shoulders, shouldering, shouldered

**shouldn't**

> This is short for *should not*. Put the apostrophe between the *n* and the *t*

**shout** *noun* shouts

**shout** *verb* shouts, shouting, shouted

**show** *noun* shows

**show** *verb* shows, showing, showed, shown

**shower** *noun* showers

**shower** *verb* showers, showering, showered

**shut** *verb* shuts, shutting, shut

**shy** *adjective* shyer or shier, shyest or shiest

**shy** *noun* shies

**shy** *verb* shies, shying, shied

**sick** *adjective* sicker, sickest

**side** *noun* sides

**side** *verb* sides, siding, sided

**sight** *noun* sights

**sight** *verb* sights, sighting, sighted

Do not confuse the spellings of *sight* and *site*: *The bombed city was a terrible sight; the site of a battle in World War One*

**sign** *noun* signs

**sign** *verb* signs, signing, signed

**signature\*** *noun* signatures

**silence** *noun* silences

**silence** *verb* silences, silencing, silenced

**silent** *adjective*

**silk** *noun* silks

**silly** *adjective* sillier, silliest

**silver** *noun*

**simple** *adjective* simpler, simplest

**sincere** *adjective*

**sincerely** *adverb*

**sing** *verb* sings, singing, sang, sung

Remember that the past tense of *sing* is *sang*

**singer** *noun* singers

**single** *noun* singles

**single** *verb* singles, singling, singled

**singular\*** *noun* singulars

**sink** *verb* sinks, sinking, sank, sunk

**sir** *noun* sirs

**sister** *noun* sisters

**sit** *verb* sits, sitting, sat

**site** *noun* sites

**site** *verb* sites, siting, sited

**situation\*** *noun* situations

**six** *noun* sixes

**sixteen** *noun* sixteens

**sixteenth** *noun* sixteenths

**sixth** *noun* sixths

**sixtieth** *noun* sixtieths

**sixty** *noun* sixties

**size** *noun* sizes

**size** *verb* sizes, sizing, sized

**skate** *noun* skates

**skate** *verb* skates, skating, skated

**skateboard** *noun* skateboards

**skateboard** *verb* skateboards, skateboarding, skateboarded

**skateboarder** *noun* skateboarders

**ski** *noun* skis

**ski** *verb* skis, skiing, skied

**skill** *noun* skills

**skin** *noun* skins

**skin** *verb* skins, skinning, skinned

**skirt** *noun* skirts

**skirt** *verb* skirts, skirting, skirted

**sky** *noun* skies

**sleep** *noun* sleeps

**sleep** *verb* sleeps, sleeping, slept

**sleepy** *adjective* sleepier, sleepiest

**sleeve** *noun* sleeves

**slice** *noun* slices

**slice** *verb* slices, slicing, sliced

**slim** *adjective* slimmer, slimmest

**slip** *noun* slips

**slip** *verb* slips, slipping, slipped

**slow** *adjective* slower, slowest

**slow** *verb* slows, slowing, slowed

# Dictionary

**small** *adjective* smaller, smallest

**smart** *adjective* smarter, smartest

**smart** *verb* smarts, smarting, smarted

**smell** *noun* smells

**smell** *verb* smells, smelling, smelt or smelled

**smile** *noun* smiles

**smile** *verb* smiles, smiling, smiled

**smoke** *noun* smokes

**smoke** *verb* smokes, smoking, smoked

**smooth** *adjective* smoother, smoothest

**smooth** *verb* smooths, smoothing, smoothed

**SMS** *noun* SMSs

**snack** *noun* snacks

**snack** *verb* snacks, snacking, snacked

**snake** *noun* snakes

**snow** *noun* snows

**snow** *verb* snows, snowing, snowed

**snowboard** *noun* snowboards

**snowstorm** *noun* snowstorms

**soap** *noun* soaps

**soap** *verb* soaps, soaping, soaped

**social** *adjective*

**society*** *noun* societies

**sock** *noun* socks

**sofa** *noun* sofas

**soft** *adjective* softer, softest

**soldier** *noun* soldiers

**soldier** *verb* soldiers, soldiering, soldiered

**solution** *noun* solutions

**solve** *verb* solves, solving, solved

**somebody** *noun* somebodies

**son** *noun* sons

**song** *noun* songs

**soon** *adjective* sooner, soonest

**sore** *noun* sores

**sore** *adjective* sorer, sorest

**sorry** *adjective* sorrier, sorriest

**sort** *noun* sorts

**sort** *verb* sorts, sorting, sorted

**soul** *noun* souls

**sound** *adjective* sounder, soundest

**sound** *noun* sounds

**sound** *verb* sounds, sounding, sounded

**soup** *noun* soups

**sour** *adjective* sourer, sourest

**sour** *verb* sours, souring, soured

**south** *noun*

**sow** *verb* sows, sowing, sowed

Do not confuse *sow* with *sew*. To *sow* is to put seed into the ground. To *sew* is to work with a thread and needle

**souvenir*** *noun* souvenirs

**space** *noun* spaces

**space** *verb* spaces, spacing, spaced

**spare** *noun* spares

**spare** *verb* spares, sparing, spared

**speak** *verb* speaks, speaking, spoke, spoken

**speaker** *noun* speakers

**special** *adjective*

**spectacular*** *noun* spectaculars

**speech** *noun* speeches

**speed** *noun* speeds

**speed** *verb* speeds, speeding, sped or speeded

**spell** *noun* spells

**spell** *verb* spells, spelling, spelt or spelled

**spelling** *noun* spellings

**spend** *verb* spends, spending, spent

**spice** *noun* spices

**spice** *verb* spices, spicing, spiced

**spicy** *adjective* spicier, spiciest

**spider** *noun* spiders

**spill** *noun* spills

**spill** *verb* spills, spilling, spilt or spilled

**spoil** *verb* spoils, spoiling, spoilt or spoiled

**spoke** *noun* spokes

**spoon** *noun* spoons

**spoon** *verb* spoons, spooning, spooned

**sport** *noun* sports

**spot** *noun* spots

**spot** *verb* spots, spotting, spotted

**spring** *verb* springs, springing, sprang, sprung

**spy** *noun* spies

**spy** *verb* spies, spying, spied

**square** *noun* squares

**square** *verb* squares, squaring, squared

**squash** *noun* squashes

**squash** *verb* squashes, squashing, squashed

**stadium** *noun* stadiums

**staff** *verb* staffs, staffing, staffed

**stage** *noun* stages

**stage** *verb* stages, staging, staged

**stair** *noun* stairs

> Do not confuse *stair* with *stare*. A *stair* is one of a set of steps. If you *stare* at something you look at it

**stake** *noun* stakes

> Do not confuse *stake* with *steak*. A *stake* is a pointed wooded post. A *steak* is a thick slice of meat

**stake** *verb* stakes, staking, staked

**stall** *noun* stalls

**stall** *verb* stalls, stalling, stalled

**stamp** *noun* stamps

**stamp** *verb* stamps, stamping, stamped

**stand** *noun* stands

**stand** *verb* stands, standing, stood

**star** *noun* stars

**star** *verb* stars, starring, starred

**stare** *noun* stares

**stare** *verb* stares, staring, stared

**start** *noun* starts

**start** *verb* starts, starting, started

**station** *noun* stations

**station** *verb* stations, stationing, stationed

**stationary*** *adjective*

**stationery*** *noun*

> Do not confuse the spellings of *stationery* and *stationary*. *Stationery* is envelopes and paper. *Stationary* means not moving

**statue** *noun* statues

> Do not confuse the spellings of *statue* and *statute*: *a marble statue of the Roman goddess Venus; an anti-terrorism statute passed by the Russian parliament*

**statute** *noun* statutes

**stay** *noun* stays

**stay** *verb* stays, staying, stayed

**steak** *noun* steaks

> Do not confuse *steak* with *stake*. A *steak* is a thick slice of meat. A *stake* is a pointed wooded post.

**steal** *verb* steals, stealing, stole, stolen

> Do not confuse the spellings of *steal* and *steel*: *He is accused of stealing a car; The government is steeling itself to take action*

> Remember that the past tense of *steal* is *stole*

**steel** *verb* steels, steeling, steeled

**steep** *adjective* steeper, steepest

**steep** *verb* steeps, steeping, steeped

# Dictionary

**step** *noun* steps

**step** *verb* steps, stepping, stepped

**stick** *noun* sticks

**stick** *verb* sticks, sticking, stuck

**sticky** *adjective* stickier, stickiest

**still** *adjective* stiller, stillest

**still** *noun* stills

**stir** *noun* stirs

**stir** *verb* stirs, stirring, stirred

**stole** *noun* stoles

**stomach\*** *noun* stomachs

**stomach\*** *verb* stomachs, stomaching, stomached

**stone** *noun* stones

**stone** *verb* stones, stoning, stoned

**stop** *noun* stops

**stop** *verb* stops, stopping, stopped

**store** *noun* stores

**store** *verb* stores, storing, stored

**storey** *noun* storeys

> Do not confuse *storey* with *story*. A *storey* is a level of a building: *My office is on the third storey*. A *story* is something you read in a book: *a book of adventure stories*

**storm** *noun* storms

**storm** *verb* storms, storming, stormed

**straight** *adjective* straighter, straightest

**story** *noun* stories

**straight** *adjective* straighter, straightest

> Do not confuse the spellings of *straight* and *strait*: *a straight line; the Strait of Messina*

**strait** *noun* straits

**strange** *adjective* strange, strangest

**stranger** *noun* strangers

**strawberry** *noun* strawberries

**stream** *noun* streams

**stream** *verb* streams, streaming, streamed

**street** *noun* streets

**streetlamp** *noun* streetlamps

**strength** *noun* strengths

**stress** *noun* stresses

**stress** *verb* stresses, stressing, stressed

**strict** *adjective* stricter, strictest

**strike** *noun* strikes

**strike** *verb* strikes, striking, struck

**strip** *noun* strips

**strip** *verb* strips, stripping, stripped

**stripe** *noun* stripes

**strong** *adjective* stronger, strongest

**student** *noun* students

**studio** *noun* studios

**study** *noun* studies

**study** *verb* studies, studying, studied

**stuff** *verb* stuffs, stuffing, stuffed

**stupid** *adjective* stupider, stupidest

**style** *noun* styles

**style** *verb* styles, styling, styled

**subject** *noun* subjects

**subject** *verb* subjects, subjecting, subjected

**subtract** *verb* subtracts, subtracting, subtracted

**subtraction\*** *noun* subtractions

**succeed** *verb* succeeds, succeeding, succeeded

**success** *noun* successes

**suffer** *verb* suffers, suffering, suffered

**sufficient** *adjective*

**sugar** *noun* sugars

**suggest** *verb* suggests, suggesting, suggested

**suggestion\*** *noun* suggestions

**suit** *noun* suits

**suit** *verb* suits, suiting, suited

**suitcase** *noun* suitcases

**summer** *noun* summers

**sun** *verb* suns, sunning, sunned

**sunbathe** *verb* sunbathes, sunbathing, sunbathed

**Sunday** *noun* Sundays

**sunk** *verb*

**sunny** *adjective* sunnier, sunniest

**sunrise** *noun* sunrises

**sunset** *noun* sunsets

**sunshine** *noun*

**superlative\*** *noun* superlatives

**supermarket** *noun* supermarkets

**supper** *noun* suppers

**support** *noun* supports

**support** *verb* supports, supporting, supported

**supporter** *noun* supporters

**suppose** *verb* supposing, supposed

Do not confuse *suppose* with *supposed to*. *Suppose* is a verb. If you *suppose* that something is true, you think it is probably true: *I suppose it was difficult*. If something is *supposed to* be done, it should be done because of a rule or instruction: *I'm not supposed to talk to you about this*. If something is *supposed to* be true, most people think it is true: *It's supposed to be a good movie*

**sure** *adjective* surer, surest

**surf** *noun* surfs

**surf** *verb* surfs, surfing, surfed

**surfer** *noun* surfers

**surname** *noun* surnames

**surprise** *noun* surprises

**surprise** *verb* surprises, surprising, surprised

**surround** *noun* surrounds

**surround** *verb* surrounds, surrounding, surrounded

**sweater** *noun* sweaters

**sweet** *adjective* sweeter, sweetest

**sweet** *noun* sweets

**swim** *verb* swims, swimming, swam, swum

Remember that the past tense of *swim* is *swam* and the past participle is *swum*

**swimmer** *noun* swimmers

**swimsuit** *noun* swimsuits

**switch** *noun* switches

**switch** *verb* switches, switching, switched

**symbol\*** *noun* symbols

**system** *noun* systems

# Tt

**table** *noun* tables

**table** *verb* tables, tabling, tabled

**tablet** *noun* tablets

**tail** *noun* tails

**tail** *verb* tails, tailing, tailed

Do not confuse *tail* with *tale*. A *tail* is a part at the back of some animals. A *tale* is a story

**take** *noun* takes

**take** *verb* takes, taking, took, taken

**takeaway** *noun* takeaways

**takeoff** *noun* takeoffs

**tale** *noun* tales

**talent** *noun* talents

**talk** *noun* talks

**talk** *verb* talks, talking, talked

**tall** *adjective* taller, tallest

**tap** *noun* taps

**tap** *verb* taps, tapping, tapped

**tart** *noun* tarts

**taste** *noun* tastes

**taste** *verb* tastes, tasting, tasted

**tasty** *adjective* tastier, tastiest

**tax** *noun* taxes

**tax** *verb* taxes, taxing, taxed

**taxi** *noun* taxis

**taxi** *verb* taxis, taxiing, taxied

**tea** *noun* teas

**teach** *verb* teaches, teaching, taught

**teacher** *noun* teachers

**teaching** *noun* teachings

**teacup** *noun* teacups

**team** *noun* teams

**team** *verb* teams, teaming, teamed

> Do not confuse *team* with *teem*. A *team* is a group of people playing together in a sport. *Teem* means to pour down

**tear** *noun* tears

**tear** *verb* tears, tearing, tore, torn

> Remember that the past tense of *tear* is *tore* and the past participle is *torn*

**teem** *verb* teems, teeming, teemed

**technique\*** *noun* techniques

**technology** *noun* technologies

**teenager** *noun* teenagers

**telephone** *noun* telephones

**telephone** *verb* telephones, telephoning, telephoned

**television\*** *noun* televisions

**tell** *noun* tells

**tell** *verb* tells, telling, told

> Remember that the past tense of *tell* is *told*

**temperature\*** *noun* temperatures

**temporary\*** *adjective*

**ten** *noun* tens

**tense** *adjective* tenser, tensest

**tense** *noun* tenses

**tense** *verb* tenses, tensing, tensed

**tent** *noun* tents

**tenth** *noun* tenths

**term** *noun* terms

**term** *verb* terms, terming, termed

**test** *noun* tests

**test** *verb* tests, testing, tested

**text** *noun* texts

**text** *verb* texts, texting, texted

**thank** *verb* thanks, thanking, thanked

**that** *determiner*

**theatre** *noun* theatres

**their** *determiner*

> Do not confuse the spellings of *their*, *there* and *they're*: *Their house is the blue one; That's my car over there; They're always late*

**there** *adverb*

> A good way to remember that *there* is connected to the idea of place is by remembering the spelling of two other place words: *here* and *where*

**therefore** *adverb*

**they'd**

> This is short for *they would* or *they had*. Put the apostrophe between the *y* and the *d*

**they'll**

> This is short for *they will*. Put the apostrophe between the *y* and the first *l*

**they're**

> This is short for *they are*. Put the apostrophe between the *y* and the *r*

**they've**

> This is short for *they have*. Put the apostrophe between the *y* and the *v*

**thick** *adjective* thicker, thickest

**thief** *noun* thieves

**thin** *adjective* thinner, thinnest

**thin** *verb* thins, thinning, thinned

**thing** *noun* things

**think** *verb* thinks, thinking, thought

> Remember that the past tense is *thought*

**third** *noun* thirds

**thirsty** *adjective* thirstier, thirstiest

**thirteen** *noun* thirteens

**thirteenth** *noun* thirteenths

**thirtieth** *noun* thirtieths

**thirty** *noun* thirties

**thorough** *adjective*

**though** *conjunction*

**thought** *noun* thoughts

**thousand** *noun* thousands

**thousandth** *noun* thousandths

**three** *noun* threes

**thriller** *noun* thrillers

**throat** *noun* throats

**through** *preposition*

> Do not confuse the spellings of *through* and *threw* (the past tense of *throw*): *The river runs through the centre of town; Aidan threw the ball over the fence*

**throw** *noun* throws

**throw** *verb* throws, throwing, threw, thrown

**thumb** *noun* thumbs

**thumb** *verb* thumbs, thumbing, thumbed

**thunderstorm** *noun* thunderstorms

**Thursday** *noun* Thursdays

**tick** *noun* ticks

**tick** *verb* ticks, ticking, ticked

**ticket** *noun* tickets

**ticket** *verb* tickets, ticketing, ticketed

**tidy** *adjective* tidier, tidiest

**tidy** *verb* tidies, tidying, tidied

**tie** *noun* ties

**tie** *verb* ties, tying, tied

**tiger** *noun* tigers

**tight** *adjective* tighter, tightest

**till** *noun* tills

**till** *verb* tills, tilling, tilled

**time** *noun* times

**time** *verb* times, timing, timed

**timetable** *noun* timetables

**tin** *noun* tins

**tin** *verb* tins, tinning, tinned

**tiny** *adjective* tinier, tiniest

**tip** *noun* tips

**tip** *verb* tips, tipping, tipped

**tire** *noun* tires

**tire** *verb* tires, tiring, tired

> Do not confuse the spellings of *tire* and *tyre*: *Since my illness I tire easily; Jonny's car needs a new front tyre*

**tissue** *noun* tissues

**title** *noun* titles

**title** *verb* titles, titling, titled

**to** *preposition*

> The preposition *to* is spelt with one *o*, the adverb *too* has two *os*, and the number *two* is spelt with *wo*

**toast** *noun* toasts

**toast** *verb* toasts, toasting, toasted

**toaster** *noun* toasters

**toe** *noun* toes

> Do not confuse *toe* with *tow*. A *toe* is part of a foot. To *tow* something means to pull it along

**toilet** *noun* toilets

**tomato** *noun* tomatoes

**tomorrow*** *noun* tomorrows

**tongue*** *noun* tongues

**too** *adverb*

**tooth** *noun* teeth

**toothache** *noun* toothaches

**toothbrush** *noun* toothbrushes

**toothpaste** *noun* toothpastes

**top** *noun* tops

**top** *verb* tops, topping, topped

**topic** *noun* topics

**tore** *verb*

**total** *noun* totals

**total** *verb* totals, totalling, totalled

**touch** *noun* touches

**touch** *verb* touches, touching, touched

**tour** *noun* tours

**tour** *verb* tours, touring, toured

**tourist** *noun* tourists

**tournament** *noun* tournaments

**tow** *noun* tows

**tow** *verb* tows, towing, towed

> Do not confuse *tow* with toe. To *tow* something means to pull it along. A *toe* is part of a foot

**towel** *noun* towels

**towel** *verb* towels, towelling, towelled

**tower** *noun* towers

**tower** *verb* towers, towering, towered

**town** *noun* towns

**toy** *noun* toys

**toy** *verb* toys, toying, toyed

**track** *noun* tracks

**track** *verb* tracks, tracking, tracked

**trade** *noun* trades

**trade** *verb* trades, trading, traded

**traffic** *verb* traffics, trafficking, trafficked

**train** *noun* trains

**train** *verb* trains, training, trained

**trainer** *noun* trainers

**tram** *noun* trams

**transfer** *noun* transfers

**transfer** *verb* transfers, transferring, transferred

**translate** *verb* translates, translating, translated

**translation** *noun* translations

**transport** *noun* transports

**transport** *verb* transports, transporting, transported

**transportation\*** *noun*

**trash** *verb* trashes, trashing, trashed

**travel** *noun* travels

**travel** *verb* travels, travelling, travelled

**traveller** *noun* travellers

**tree** *noun* trees

**trend** *noun* trends

**trick** *noun* tricks

**trick** *verb* tricks, tricking, tricked

**trip** *noun* trips

**trip** *verb* trips, tripping, tripped

**triple** *noun* triples

**triple** *verb* triples, tripling, tripled

**trouble** *noun* troubles

**trouble** *verb* troubles, troubling, troubled

**truck** *noun* trucks

**true** *adjective* truer, truest

**truly** *adverb*

**trumpet** *noun* trumpets

**trumpet** *verb* trumpets, trumpeting, trumpeted

**trunk** *noun* trunks

**trust** *noun* trusts

**trust** *verb* trusts, trusting, trusted

**truth** *noun* truths

**try** *noun* tries

**try** *verb* tries, trying, tried

> Remember that the past tense of *try* is *tried*

**T-shirt** *noun* T-shirts

**tube** *noun* tubes

**Tuesday** *noun* Tuesdays

**tummy** *noun* tummies

**tuna** *noun* tuna, tunas

**tune** *noun* tunes

**tune** *verb* tunes, tuning, tuned

**tunnel** *noun* tunnels

**tunnel** *verb* tunnels, tunnelling, tunnelled

**turkey** *noun* turkeys

**turn** *noun* turns

**turn** *verb* turns, turning, turned

**turning** *noun* turnings

**TV** *noun* TVs

**twelfth** *noun* twelfths

**twelve** *noun* twelves

**twentieth** *noun* twentieths

**twenty** *noun* twenties

**twin** *noun* twins

**twin** *verb* twins, twinning, twinned

**two** *noun* twos

> Do not confuse the spelling of the preposition *to*, the adverb *too*, and the number *two*

**type** *noun* types

**type** *verb* types, typing, typed

**tyre** *noun* tyres

> Do not confuse the spellings of *tyre* and *tire*: Jonny's car needs a new front tyre; Since my illness I tire easily

# Uu

**ugly** *adjective* uglier, ugliest

**umbrella** *noun* umbrellas

**uncle** *noun* uncles

**underground** *noun* undergrounds

**underline** *verb* underlines, underlining, underlined

**understand** *verb* understands, understanding, understood

**undress** *verb* undresses, undressing, undressed

**unfit** *adjective*

**unfriendly** *adjective* unfriendlier, unfriendliest

**unhappy** *adjective* unhappier, unhappiest

**unhealthy** *adjective* unhealthier, unhealthiest

**uniform** *noun* uniforms

**union** *noun* unions

**unit** *noun* units

**universe** *noun* universes

**university** *noun* universities

**unkind** *adjective* unkinder, unkindest

**unknown** *adjective*

**unlikely** *adjective* unlikelier, unlikeliest

**unlucky** *adjective* unluckier, unluckiest

**unpack** *verb* unpacks, unpacking, unpacked

**untidy** *adjective* untidier, untidiest

**upload** *verb* uploads, uploading, uploaded

**upper** *noun* uppers

**upset** *noun* upsets

**upset** *verb* upsets, upsetting, upset

**use** *noun* uses

**use** *verb* uses, using, used

**useful** *adjective*

**user** *noun* users

**usual** *adjective*

**usually** *adverb*

# Vv

**vain** *adjective* vainer, vainest

> Do not confuse the spellings of *vain*, *vane* and *vein*. *Vain* means proud or conceited. A *vane* shows which way the wind is blowing. A *vein* carries blood to the heart

**valley** *noun* valleys

**valuable** *adjective*

**value** *noun* values

**value** *verb* values, valuing, valued

**van** *noun* vans

**vane** *noun* vanes

**variety*** *noun* varieties

**various** *adjective*

**vase** *noun* vases
**vegetable** *noun* vegetables
**vegetarian*** *noun* vegetarians
**vehicle*** *noun* vehicles
**vein** *noun* veins
**verb** *noun* verbs
**vet** *noun* vets
**vet** *verb* vets, vetting, vetted
**veterinary*** *adjective*
**video** *noun* videos
**video** *verb* videos, videoing, videoed
**view** *noun* views
**view** *verb* views, viewing, viewed
**village** *noun* villages
**violin** *noun* violins
**virus** *noun* viruses
**visa** *noun* visas
**visit** *noun* visits
**visit** *verb* visits, visiting, visited
**visitor** *noun* visitors
**visual** *adjective*
**vocabulary*** *noun* vocabularies
**voice** *noun* voices
**voice** *verb* voices, voicing, voiced
**volleyball** *noun* volleyballs
**volume** *noun* volumes
**voluntary** *adjective*
**volunteer** *noun* volunteers

**volunteer** *verb* volunteers, volunteering, volunteered
**vote** *noun* votes
**vote** *verb* votes, voting, voted
**vowel** *noun* vowels

# Ww

**wage** *noun* wages
**wage** *verb* wages, waging, waged
**waist** *noun* waists

Do not confuse *waist* with *waste*. Your *waist* is the middle part of your body. To *waste* something is to use more of it than necessary

**wait** *noun* waits
**wait** *verb* waits, waiting, waited

Do not confuse *wait* with *weight*. To *wait* is to rest or pause. The *weight* of something is how heavy it is

**waiter** *noun* waiters
**waitress** *noun* waitresses
**waive** *verb* waives, waiving, waived

Do not confuse the spellings of *waive* and *wave*: All the bands in the concert have waived their fees; Aileen looked over and waved at me

**wake** *noun* wakes
**wake** *verb* wakes, waking, woke, woken

Remember that the past tense of *wake* is *woke* and the past participle is *woken*

**walk** *noun* walks
**walk** *verb* walks, walking, walked
**wall** *noun* walls
**wallet** *noun* wallets
**wander** *verb* wanders, wandering, wandered

Do not confuse the spellings of *wander* and *wonder*: We wandered through the gardens; I wondered why she had been trying to contact me

**want** *noun* wants
**want** *verb* wants, wanting, wanted
**war** *noun* wars
**war** *verb* wars, warring, warred
**wardrobe** *noun* wardrobes
**warm** *adjective* warmer, warmest
**warm** *verb* warms, warming, warmed
**warn** *verb* warns, warning, warned
**warning** *noun* warnings
**wash** *noun* washes

**wash** *verb* washes, washing, washed

**wasn't**

This is short for *was not*. Put the apostrophe between the *n* and the *t*

**waste** *noun* wastes

**waste** *verb* wastes, wasting, wasted

Do not confuse *waste* with *waist*. To *waste* something is to use more of it than necessary. Your *waist* is the middle part of your body

**watch** *noun* watches

**watch** *verb* watches, watching, watched

**water** *noun* waters

**water** *verb* waters, watering, watered

**waterfall** *noun* waterfalls

**wave** *noun* waves

**wave** *verb* waves, waving, waved

Do not confuse the spellings of *wave* and *waive*: *Aileen looked over and waved to me; All the bands in the concert have waived their fees*

**way** *noun* ways

Do not confuse the spellings of *way* and *weigh*: *What is the quickest way to Woodfarm from here?; Weigh your ingredients carefully*

**weak** *adjective* weaker, weakest

**wear** *verb* wears, wearing, wore, worn

Remember that the past tense is *wore* and the past participle is *worn*

**weather** *noun*

Do not confuse *weather* with *whether*. *Weather* is a noun we use to talk about rain, snow, sun, etc: *The weather was great in Italy*. *Whether* is a conjunction used to talk about a choice or doubt between two or more things: *I can't decide whether to have soup or salad*

**web** *noun* webs

**webcam** *noun* webcams

**we'd**

This is short for *we would* or *we had*. Put the apostrophe between the *e* and the *d*

**wedding** *noun* weddings

**Wednesday** *noun* Wednesdays

Spelling tip: Joe WED NESsa on WEDNESday

**week** *noun* weeks

**weekday** *noun* weekdays

**weekend** *noun* weekends

**weekly** *noun* weeklies

**weigh** *verb* weighs, weighing, weighed

**weight** *noun* weights

Do not confuse *weight* with *wait*. The *weight* of something is how heavy it is. To *wait* is to rest or pause

**welcome** *noun* welcomes

**welcome** *verb* welcomes, welcoming, welcomed

**well** *adverb* better, best

**well** *noun* wells

**we'll**

This is short for *we will*. Put the apostrophe between the *e* and the first *l*

**were** *verb*

Were is the past tense of *be* when the subject is plural: *We were very happy*

Do not confuse *were* and *we're*: *They were going to tell you; We're not leaving until we get paid*

**we're**

This is short for *we are*. Put the apostrophe between the first *e* and the *r*

**weren't**

This is short for *were not*. Put the apostrophe between the *n* and the *t*

**west** *noun*

**wet** *adjective* wetter, wettest

**wet** *verb* wets, wetting, wet or wetted

**we've**

This is short for *we have*. Put the apostrophe between the first *e* and the *v*

**whale** *noun* whales

**what** *determiner*

**wheelchair** *noun* wheelchairs

**when** *adverb*

**where** *adverb*

**whether\*** *conjunction*

Do not confuse *whether* with *weather*. *Weather* is a noun we use to talk about rain, snow, sun, etc: *The weather was great in Italy*. *Whether* is a conjunction used to talk about a choice or doubt between two or more things: *I can't decide whether to have soup or salad*

**which** *determiner*

Do not confuse *which* and *witch*. *Which* is used to ask questions: *Which one is mine?* A *witch* is a woman who uses witchcraft

**while** *conjunction*

**white** *adjective* whiter, whitest

**white** *noun* whites

**whiteboard** *noun* whiteboards

**who'd**

This is short for *who would*. Put the apostrophe between the *o* and the *d*

**whole** *noun* wholes

Do not confuse the spellings of *whole* and *hole*: *Emily was away for the whole of July; You have a hole in your sock*

**who'll**

This is short for *who will*. Put the apostrophe between the *o* and the first *l*

**who's**

Do not confuse *who's* and *whose*: *Who's next in line?; Whose hat is this?*

*Who's* is short for *who is* or *who has*. Put the apostrophe between the *o* and the *s*

**whose** *determiner*

**why** *adverb*

**wide** *adjective* wider, widest

**wife** *noun* wives

**wild** *adjective* wilder, wildest

**wild** *noun* wilds

**will** *noun* wills

**will** *verb* wills, willing, willed

**win** *noun* wins

**win** *verb* wins, winning, won

**wind** *noun* winds

**wind** *verb* winds, winding, winded

**wind** *verb* winds, winding, wound

The verb forms for *wind* (to cause someone to be short of breath) are *winds*, *winding* and *winded*. The verb forms for *wind* (to coil or wrap around) are *winds*, *winding* and *wound*

**window** *noun* windows

**windscreen** *noun* windscreens

**windy** *adjective* windier, windiest

**wine** *noun* wines

**wine** *verb* wines, wining, wined

**wing** *noun* wings

**winner** *noun* winners

**winter** *noun* winters

**wish** *noun* wishes

**wish** *verb* wishes, wishing, wished

**witch** *noun* witches

Do not confuse *witch* and *which*. A *witch* is a woman who uses witchcraft. *Which* is used to ask questions: *Which one is mine?*

**woman** *noun* women

**won** *verb*

Do not confuse the spellings of *won* and *one*. *Won* is the past tense of *win*. *One* is a number

**wonder** *noun* wonders

**wonder** *verb* wonders, wondering, wondered

Do not confuse the spellings of *wonder* and *wander*: *I wondered why she had been trying to contact me; We wandered through the gardens*

**won't**

This is short for *will not*. Put the apostrophe between the *n* and the *t*

**wood** *noun* woods

Do not confuse *wood* and *would*: *Would you like to come for lunch?; We collected some wood for the bonfire; They walked into the woods*

**wool** *noun* wools

**word** *noun* words

**work** *noun* works

**work** *verb* works, working, worked

**workbook** *noun* workbooks

**worker** *noun* workers

**working** *noun* workings

**workout** *noun* workouts

**worksheet** *noun* worksheets

**world** *noun* worlds

**worry** *noun* worries

**worry** *verb* worries, worrying, worried

**worth** *noun*

**would** *verb*

**wouldn't**

This is short for *would not*. Put the apostrophe between the *n* and the *t*

**wow** *interjection*

**wrap** *noun* wraps

**wrap** *verb* wraps, wrapping, wrapped

Do not confuse the spellings of *wrap* and *rap*: *I have wrapped all my Christmas presents; The teacher rapped the table with a ruler*

**wreck** *noun* wrecks

**wreck** *verb* wrecks, wrecking, wrecked

**write** *verb* writes, writing, wrote, written

Do not confuse the spellings of *write, right* and *rite*: *Write your name on the jotter; Is that the right answer?; the marriage rites of the Christian church*

Remember that the past tense of *write* is *wrote*

**writer** *noun* writers

**writing** *noun* writings

**wrong** *noun* wrongs

**wrong** *verb* wrongs, wronging, wronged

# Yy

**yacht** *noun* yachts

**yard** *noun* yards

**year** *noun* years

**yearly** *adjective*

**yellow** *adjective* yellower, yellowest

**yellow** *noun* yellows

**yellow** *verb* yellows, yellowing, yellowed

**yes** *interjection*

**yesterday** *noun* yesterdays

**yoga** *noun*

**yogurt** *noun* yogurts

**you'd**

This is short for *you would* or *you had*. Put the apostrophe between the *u* and the *d*

**you'll**

This is short for *you will*. Put the apostrophe between the *u* and the first *l*

**young** *adjective* younger, youngest

**your** *determiner*

Do not confuse the spellings of *your* and *you're*. *Your* is a determiner showing possession and *you're* is short for *you are*: *Don't forget your phone; You're joking, aren't you?*

**you're**

This is short for *you are*. Put the apostrophe between the *u* and the *r*

**yourself** *pronoun* yourselves

**youth** *noun* youths

**you've**

This is short for *you have*. Put the apostrophe between the *u* and the *v*

# Zz

**zero** *noun* zeros or zeroes

**zero** *verb* zeroes, zeroing, zeroed

**zone** *noun* zones

**zone** *verb* zones, zoning, zoned

**zoo** *noun* zoos

# Index

# Index

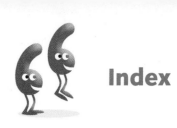

# Index

# Index